Japanese Ru

Sebastian Moffett has spent most of his adult life in Japan, and has an MA in Japanese studies from London University's School of Oriental and African Studies. Since 1990 he has worked as a correspondent for Reuters, the *Far Eastern Economic Review* and *Time* magazine.

JAPANESE RULES

*Why the Japanese Needed Football
and How They Got It*

SEBASTIAN MOFFETT

YELLOW JERSEY PRESS
LONDON

Published by Yellow Jersey Press 2003

2 4 6 8 10 9 7 5 3 1

First published in Great Britain in 2002 by
Yellow Jersey Press

Yellow Jersey Press
Random House, 20 Vauxhall Bridge Road,
London SW1V 2SA

Random House Australia (Pty) Limited
20 Alfred Street, Milsons Point, Sydney,
New South Wales 2061, Australia

Random House New Zealand Limited
18 Poland Road, Glenfield,
Auckland 10, New Zealand

Random House (Pty) Limited
Endulini, 5A Jubilee Road, Parktown 2193, South Africa

Random House UK Limited Reg. No. 954009
www.randomhouse.co.uk

A CIP catalogue record for this book
is available from the British Library

ISBN 0-224-06206-9

Papers used by Random House UK Limited are natural,
recyclable products made from wood grown in sustainable forests;
the manufacturing processes conform to the environmental
regulations of the country of origin.

Typeset by Deltatype Ltd, Birkenhead, Merseyside

Printed and bound in Great Britain by
Cox & Wyman Ltd, Reading, Berkshire

CONTENTS

PROLOGUE

Grass

It was the grass that struck him first. As he ran, it felt like springs beneath his feet. To touch, it was softer and thicker than any grass he had felt before. When he tripped up, it cushioned his fall like a carpet. But most of all, it made him want to play more football.

In the summer of 1960, while the rest of the world watched the Rome Olympic Games, Saburo Kawabuchi was training with the other members of the Japan football team in the suburbs of Duisburg, West Germany. They had failed to qualify for these Olympics, but the next Games were scheduled for Tokyo, and Japan would qualify automatically as hosts. The Tokyo Games would serve as a coming-out party for a nation pulling itself out of the ruins and shame of war defeat, and national pride demanded they not be humiliated. So a young Japanese football team was travelling round Europe to test themselves against better opposition.

They lost 6–1 to a select eleven from England's amateur Isthmian league, and 8–0 to a team in the Soviet Union. More than the quality of European football, however, Kawabuchi was impressed by the location for the training camp in Duisburg – a *Sportschule*, a kind of giant sports centre. He was stunned. Teams ranging from young boys to the middle-aged played on nine grass football pitches. Parents exercised with their children in three gymnasiums, or rowed boats on a pond. Afterwards they washed off in the showers or baths, then ate in the restaurant. They could watch a film in the cinema and stay overnight in one of the guestrooms. The football pitches were separated by lines of trees decorated by rabbits darting around their trunks.

Japan had sports teams, but they represented either

I

universities, like Kawabuchi's, or corporations: Furukawa Electric was the strongest in football, followed by Dunlop Japan. And even these teams had hardly anywhere to play. Japan's native grass grew in the hot, wet summers, but turned brown and all but disappeared in winter. Football teams played on gravel or earth pitches, with potholes that made it almost impossible to pass the ball accurately. As a result Japanese footballers mainly hoofed the ball from one end of the pitch to the other. 'Even if you can't have grass to play on,' suggested a German coach who visited Japan after meeting the team in Duisburg, 'it wouldn't be so bad if the grounds were at least rolled flat once a week. Japanese grounds are too full of bumps, putting players in danger of injury and making it extremely hard to practise.'

Playing on a grass pitch, Kawabuchi found he wanted to train for twice as long as usual. He asked how the *Sportschule* was run, and was told it was just for the use of local people – anyone who wanted to come along. 'I was shocked,' he remembered years later. 'I was even more surprised when I found out West Germany had something called the Sportschule Law, and that they were run not by corporations or the government, but by local communities. It was fantastic. I thought nothing like this could be built in Japan in a hundred years.'

Nearly forty years later, high in a central Tokyo office block, Kawabuchi opened a scrapbook of photographs and news clippings on a long glass coffee table, and described his first trip to Europe. Kawabuchi's wide smile was still the same as that of the young man beaming with confidence in the pictures, but his trim sportsman's frame had thickened out and his hair was streaked with grey. The grey hairs had mostly arrived over the past six years, a time in which he had tried to build something like he had seen in Germany. In 1993 he had set up the J.League, Japan's first professional football league, and it had been an explosive success. Hundreds of fans had stood for hours in the hope of buying tickets, a wait that often ended with them trudging home to watch matches shown live on primetime TV. After a while though, the nation had lost interest: gaps opened in the once-packed stands; football appeared less on the TV schedules; the teams started to lose money.

Kawabuchi's plan had been deliberately ambitious. When he set up the league he drew up principles and rules deliberately opposed to the previous organisation of Japanese sport – notably, he forced company teams to rename themselves after the cities they played in. He thought Japanese life was over-dominated by business, and people at least deserved sports teams representing their hometowns rather than corporations. 'The J.League is a social revolution,' Kawabuchi said. 'It's different from just making Japan good at football.'

Even if other Japanese did not talk about revolution, they seemed hungry for something football offered. Japanese football fans were always keen to point out that if it was the 'real' Japan you were after, you should go and watch baseball – the Japanese variety, of course. In the professional baseball leagues, teams like the 'Nippon Ham Fighters' played the 'Daiei Hawks' – a meat processor against a supermarket chain. The players wore grim, at-work expressions and short black hair, much like the office workers who went to see them play. In short, baseball was a reflection of the corporate way of life that had dominated Japan since the war. The people who recommended taking in some baseball added that they didn't much like the game themselves, but thought baseball was the reality of their nation, and football was somehow not really Japanese. This was, of course, the very reason they were attracted to football in the first place – it was new and had nothing to do with the grim, workaholic Japan of the economic miracle. Instead the game transported them to other worlds where people sang, lit fireworks and danced for joy. 'As soon as they get into the stadium they become John Bull, they become Germanic, they become Argentine and Brazilian,' wrote one fan of the gang he hung out with. 'In other words

3

they are Japanese living in their own country, who have abandoned a little of their Japaneseness.'

So instead of just improving its ball skills, Japan threw itself into the whole culture of football. Teams got exotic names like 'Kyoto Purple Sanga'. The players often had shaggy, brown-tinted hair and developed silly dances to celebrate goals. Japanese coaches studied in Germany, while teenagers went to Brazil to live in club dormitories in the hope of putting samba in their feet. Wise minds came to Japan to pass on knowledge from football's Old World: Brazilian stars Zico and Dunga taught players to be cunning in the South American way; England's Steve Perryman taught them how to be less friendly towards their opponents; France's intellectual coaching wizard Arsène Wenger told them to think more; Dutchman Hans Ooft told the national team to talk to each other during play; and a later national coach, Frenchman Philippe Troussier, kissed his players on the cheeks and made them sing songs after victories.

For Kawabuchi, however, all of this was subsidiary to his dream of municipal football fields and basketball courts that anyone could play on. When he became general secretary of the Japan Football Association (JFA) in 1988 and decided to start the J.League, Japan was rich – rich enough to add a new professional team sport, and rich enough, surely, to provide some play space for ordinary people. 'The Japanese had not experienced this kind of community-based sports club,' Kawabuchi explained, 'because people didn't know about them. The top people from the government and industry had been abroad and knew about how good sports clubs were, but they didn't think of setting them up in Japan. They thought, abroad is abroad and Japan is Japan, and they are different.'

Amid the glamour of a new sports league and efforts to play football like the rest of the world, Kawabuchi's ideas were somehow drowned out and forgotten by most people. Japan's national team became wildly popular, and the best of a new generation of Japanese players made it in the

Italian league, the world's toughest. But almost no sports centres were built, and fans eventually began to stay home on Saturday afternoons. In an attempt to understand why, Kawabuchi started avoiding the VIP boxes when he went to watch football each week. Instead he took a seat or stood at the home supporters' end. With his booming voice and easy laugh, he became a familiar face among the fans he talked to, and on the days he went alone they would ask after his wife and why she hadn't come that week. Some grounds pulsated with crowds of singing, chanting young fans, whose clothes and banners turned their stadiums into seas of colour. At others, the rows of empty seats produced a ghostly atmosphere. Faced with high wage bills and poor turn-outs, the two teams based in Yokohama 'merged' at the end of 1998. Soon after this, Kawabuchi contemplated his attempted revolution and sighed: 'People need to feel "This is our town's team", like they do with Barcelona or Manchester United.' He concluded: 'In some places they don't have this feeling. It's like sprinkling water in the desert.'

CHAPTER ONE

If We Build It . . .

'The Japanese worked from Meiji in order to catch up with the western nations. Then they started the same thing from zero all over again after the Second World War. But what did they work for? Surely they can't just be working in order to buy American land and real estate to make more money. It can't just be in order to stare at the bar chart of growing trade surplus and give a satisfied smile. The J.League gave a clear answer to this: We are living to enjoy sport . . . we are living to create culture.'

(Masayuki Tamaki, 1993.

A Japanese footballer's day consisted of more than just training. Takayoshi Yamano, one of the country's top centre backs of his time, started his days putting on a suit and tie and picking up a briefcase. Every morning, he arrived at his desk at heavy machinery company Yanmar Diesel at nine o'clock, got a cup of coffee and settled down to his morning work. On a busy day he might have to check some numbers. Mostly though he read football magazines and drank coffee. If the women at the desks near him weren't too busy, he'd chat to them about football. Then at eleven o'clock, he went for lunch. 'It wasn't really a job, and there wasn't anything for me to do,' he remembered later of his morning work. 'I couldn't do anything directly related to the company's business because it's not possible to do anything significant in that short time. I worked for Yanmar Kenki [the construction machine division] but I can't remember now what department or section it was.'

For Yamano, the real day started in the afternoon, when he would train at the company football ground from two until five. At the weekends he played matches against other companies, which was his real value to the company because the results appeared in the papers with the company name. Those results didn't affect his pay at all, which rose a little each year and was equal to that of other Yanmar employees who had entered the company at the same time. So though disappointed when he played badly or the team lost, it didn't spoil the beers on the train home from matches. When a player could no longer cut it out on the field, he could move on to anonymity and admin somewhere in the company.

When Yamano was picked for the national team in 1979, he decided he wanted to devote himself to football. Football was already his only useful contribution to Yanmar, and he asked the coach if he could stop his morning office 'work' to spend the time resting or training. The coach declined, so eventually he did what Japanese company employees never did in those days. He left the company for a job elsewhere – this time to a company that made an exception and paid him as a player-coach instead of making him do office work. 'I kept asking them to let me train full-time over about two years,' he remembered. 'But they always made the same reply: It was company policy.'

Company policy defined much of post-war Japanese life, and sport was no exception. Japan had no sports clubs for use by the local community and no teams representing local towns. Instead, football – along with volleyball and basketball – was played in schools, colleges and companies. Company players were full-time employees like Yamano, usually spending the morning in a factory or office, then training in the afternoon. Most lived in company dormitories, where they ate breakfast, lunch and dinner together in the canteen. More than western sport, professional or amateur, Japan's company sport resembled a capitalist version of the state-amateurism practised in eastern Europe's communist era, when Olympic victories demonstrated the might of the state that had nurtured the athletes.

It had taken a long time for football to get even this far in Japan. Football first entered the country in 1873 through a

7

British naval commander who was teaching at Tokyo's naval academy, and started kicking a ball around with students between drill. Football then spread slowly via academic institutions. The first national championship was held in 1921, following a mistaken report by a news agency. In 1919, three football tournaments were held in Japan, one in Kansai, the area of western Japan including Osaka, Kyoto and Kobe, one in the Kanto area around Tokyo, and one in Tokai, the region in-between. Though the three were independent events, the news service reported that they were regional qualifying tournaments for a national championship planned by a new Japanese football organisation. When this was read at Football Association headquarters in London, the FA sent a large silver cup to Tokyo via the British Embassy. So Japan had an FA Cup. All it needed now was an FA. On 10 September 1921, the Japan Football Association (JFA) was set up, and its first championship was held two months later in Tokyo, with the silver cup from England going to the winner. The cup was a casualty of the Second World War, however. It was lost and has since been replaced by the Emperor's Cup.

Though most western sports were introduced to Japan around the end of the nineteenth century, baseball quickly outstripped all others. One reason was a highly publicised victory in 1896 by the First Higher School of Tokyo, Japan's most elite high school, over a team of Americans from the Yokohama Country Athletic Club. But the more appealing explanation is the difference in methods of warfare between Japan and the West. The Tokugawa Shogunate that ruled Japan from 1603 to 1868 had restricted the production of guns, and the samurai instead carried swords. So instead of the long-range shots at a group of opponents, the Japanese art of war consisted of one-on-one battles. If a mass gun battle was similar in spirit to football, a sword fight resembled the conflict between a pitcher and a batter, especially considering the swinging motion of the latter. Following trips to Japan by groups of US Major League all-stars in 1931 and 1934, Japan set up its own professional baseball league in 1935. After the war baseball became far and away Japan's most popular spectator sport, dominating primetime television and newspaper sports sections.

Football, meanwhile, was a minor affair. For their first forty years, the FA and Emperor's Cups were competed for almost exclusively by college and college old-boy teams. That changed in 1960 however, when a team from electric wire manufacturer Furukawa Electric Co. became the first company team to win. Corporate sport began in the 1950s, as Japan began its post-war reconstruction. The first big company sports teams were set up by textile companies, which wanted to attract women with at least a junior high school education, but were hampered by the industry's dirty, hard-labour image. Many of the new young workers came from the countryside and lived away from home in company dormitories. To improve their morale and help them identify with their employer, companies like the Toray formed volleyball teams that played each other in a corporate league. Workers then followed their company team's progress on radio broadcasts and cinema news bulletins. At the Melbourne Olympics in 1956, company athletes outnumbered the students on Japan's Olympic team for the first time, starting a dominance that would continue for the next half century. Corporate sport's finest hour came at the 1964 Tokyo Olympics, when Japan won the women's volleyball gold medal with a team made up of textile company players.

In this era, top-level competition was only one aspect of company sport and leisure. Corporate morale and the resulting willingness to make sacrifices for an employer were big factors in the high-speed economic growth Japan began in the 1960s. Companies also organised sports days, excursions to swim at the beach and educational classes. These helped nurture a culture of company as family, and enabled employers to manage workers' leisure time.

By about 1965, Japan had recovered from its post-war hardships, and was transforming into a society that revolved around mass consumption. From this time, company sport was broadcast on television, and became a way to advertise products. In women's volleyball, consumer electronics companies like Toshiba and Hitachi – makers of TV sets, fridges and irons – began to challenge the textile companies for supremacy. As sports teams gained this kind of media value, the stakes were raised. More than uniting employees, the purpose of sports teams now was to put the company name on shirts that would be seen on TV and in newspapers. Athletes were scouted especially for the teams and in many companies had little connection with regular employees. To increase their competitiveness, some companies began hiring foreigner players, often recruiting from countries where they had branch offices so could pretend that they were simply staff from these affiliates. Like Yamano at Yanmar, they were professionals in all but name, maintaining the façade that they were corporate gentlemen who happened to be amateur sportsmen on the side. By the 1980s top companies were spending well over a million pounds a year on running their sports teams.

Football started to grow in the 1960s with the second phase of company sport – teams as advertising vehicles – and Waseda University's victory in the 1963 Emperor's Cup was the last for a college. But the biggest agent of change for Japanese football was a German coach called Dettmar Cramer, who was assigned to train the Japan team that went to the Duisburg *Sportschule* in 1960. He was small and bald and had a piercing glare. One team member, Ken Naganuma, who later became JFA chairman, remembered how 'he looked straight into my eyes ... and I thought immediately that when talking to this man I was not allowed to avert my eyes. I felt a sense of warmth towards him because he was a similar size to me, but the sternness of his eyes made a big impression.' Another, Shigeo Yaegasu, said he 'wondered if he could play football in Europe being that small'. In fact Cramer had played as a striker for Borussia Dortmund, and soon gave them an indication of how he had coped. Showing the players round a gymnasium in the *Sportschule*, he jumped to head a ball hanging from a rope, and hit it so hard it banged against the ceiling. When the ball came down again, he stopped it dead on his forehead. According to Naganuma: 'It looked really easy, but it was something that none of the Japanese national team players could manage.'

The team's initial efforts were abysmal. They lost their first match, against Alemennia Aachen, 5–0, and followed this with more crushing defeats, including an 8–0 loss to Torpedo Moscow. But Cramer saw the players were desperate to learn, and decided to continue coaching them after the *Sportschule* camp ended. 'All the players were university educated, and I was impressed by the high intellectual standard – the desire to learn,' he remembered later. 'I became really keen on teaching them myself, and started to change my schedule to get more time in Japan.'

But the more Cramer saw, the more shocked he was. He described what he saw in a variety of biting similes. Japanese players danced round the ball 'like mosquitoes round a light', he said. Teammates fought among themselves for the ball, he said, like chickens in a run who rushed headlong towards food. When one player did get the ball, he punted it up the field, after which the opposition punted it back. 'I had heard that they played football in Japan, but what I saw was ping pong,' Cramer told the players at one point. 'Just look at the faces of the people in the stands. They look right, and then they look left, then they look right again and so on.'

Despite their weaknesses, the players were determined to improve and with Cramer's guidance they gradually did. To gain match experience against stronger opposition, Cramer took the team on several tours of Europe, and invited European teams to Japan. Though they still lost much of the time, the defeats became less heavy, and were interspersed with victories. In 1963, they drew one match and won another against the German Olympic team, and the next year they beat Grasshoppers of Zurich 4–0. The aim of all this had been to avoid humiliation in the Tokyo

Olympics, and by 1964 they had come far enough. Though they lost 3–2 to Ghana and were eventually knocked out in the quarterfinals by a 4–0 loss to Czechoslovakia, they managed a victory that would have been unthinkable just a few years before: 3–2 against Argentina.

After this, Japanese football got better and better. In 1965, following a suggestion from Cramer, the JFA started the national Japan Soccer League (JSL) for company teams to replace the previous regional leagues. After the Tokyo Olympics, striker Ryuichi Sugiyama received an offer for $200,000 to play in Argentina. Though he turned it down to continue playing for his company and the national team, this confirmed that at least one Japanese player had reached professional standard.

Cramer's coaching career took him virtually everywhere. He trained 150,000 boys in Germany, including the young Franz Beckenbauer, and was part of the coaching staff of several German national teams, including the 1954 World Cup winners and the runners-up in 1966. He coached at Bayern Munich in the 1970s and in a total of over ninety countries. In 2001, at the age of seventy-six, he was spending ten months a year in China to set up a coaching certificate system (he still rose at 4.30 a.m. every morning to spend an hour maintaining his own skills). How did the Japanese compare to all the other people he had coached? 'The Japanese learned faster than anyone else,' he said. 'Their number one trait was a drive and determination to get better.'

He came to love Japan, and even enquired about naturalizing as a Japanese, though he was told that dual nationality was almost impossible to arrange. For over a decade, he spent three months of most years in Japan, teaching coaching clinics and instructing the national team. He turned down the JFA's offer of a western-style hotel during some of these camps, preferring instead to live like the players. He slept on *tatami*-mat floors, and lived off the sparse diet Japanese footballers made do with in those days – usually just a bowl of rice with vegetables, egg and sometimes chicken. He lost eight kilograms during one stay in Japan, and became so thin that his wedding ring fell down the plughole when he was washing his hands.

Cramer's role was similar to that of other foreign teachers in Japanese history, who came to help the nation with its usual way to improve at anything: import knowledge. In the Meiji era (1868–1912) when Japan embarked on a crash course in modernisation, universities employed foreign professors, the navy was developed with cooperation from Britain, and Japanese men of learning travelled the world to return with the intellectual tools of progress. The Japanese cultural ideal was summed up in a phrase that was supposed to provide the best of both worlds: '*Wakon yosai* – Japanese spirit, western learning.'

While providing the western learning, Cramer started wondering about the Japanese spirit. His father had been a landscape designer, and he grew up in a house containing books on Japanese gardens. He read widely about old Japanese culture, and developed the idea that football played in the spirit of the samurai warrior might produce magical results. At first, however, though impressed by the Japanese players' brains and hunger for knowledge, Cramer was disappointed by their hearts. They were students or salaried employees rather than professionals, and appeared afraid of getting injured. 'At first I was not happy because they were too sensitive,' he said. So Cramer started telling them he wanted to see the *Yamato damashi* – Japanese spirit: 'Before you control others, you have to fight the war against yourself,' as he explained it. 'Victory over yourself is the highest victory.' He told the players they needed to overcome their fears of injury and make sacrifices for the team. Kunishige Kamamoto, the team's standout player, remembered: 'He always told us, "You have the *Yamato damashi*." Those were the only two words of Japanese that he knew. I don't know what it is – but I think it's about fighting to the very last.'

Unlike Tokyo, where Japan were given an automatic berth, they qualified by right for the next Olympics in

Mexico City in 1968. Japan beat Nigeria and France and drew with Brazil and Spain, but then lost 5–0 to Hungary in the semi-finals. The match to decide the bronze medal pitted Japan against Mexico, and Cramer told the players to defend with all their might: the home crowd would naturally support their own team, but if they failed to score, Mexico would get anxious, and the crowd even more so. Japan went 2–0 ahead in the first half from goals by Kamamoto and, sure enough, the crowd got frustrated. Some even began to support Japan with chants of '*Japón, Japón, La La La! Japón, Japón, La La La!*' At the halftime break, a banner appeared demanding the Mexico manager leave the ground. Two minutes into the second half, Mexico missed a penalty, and this time the whole stadium began to support Japan. Japan doggedly defended their 2–0 lead, and while they were collecting their bronze medals, some Mexicans carried a replica coffin for their team manager into one of the stands, where they set it alight.

The 1968 team was the strongest Japan team yet. Kamamoto scored seven goals in six matches in the Olympics, and was the competition's top scorer. Back in the Olympic village after the Mexico game, the players were dizzy and shaking with exhaustion, and collapsed on the ground one by one. To revive them, they were given hot tea and *miso* soup, and wrapped in blankets. Decades later even Cramer said that in all of his half century of coaching, 'I have never experienced that kind of sacrifice from players.' At the time he was moved to tears – and awarding them the ultimate accolade, he announced he had 'finally seen the *Yamato damashi*'.

The bronze medal, the new generation of players and the JSL all pointed to a rosy future for Japanese football. But in fact it had just seen its finest hour for a long time. The national team failed to qualify for the Olympics, let alone the World Cup, for several more decades. Baseball got all the media exposure, and football went into a slump. Japanese football matches became a depressing sight.

Attendance at most JSL matches was no more than a few hundred, although organisers, embarrassed by the low turnouts, routinely doubled the numbers when announcing the 'official' figures. The spectators spread themselves over several seats, where they drank beer and picked at boxes of snack food with chopsticks. They kept one eye on the game happening on the thin brown grass below, but mostly chatted amongst themselves. They felt no need to get value from the matches because nearly all had received their tickets free from the team owners. There were no support songs nor chants because there were no real supporters – just people who sometimes turned up after work to see a team with the same name as their employer.

Japanese football was so hopeless that in 1977 the country's best player, Yasuhiko Okudera, left to play as a striker for FC Köln in West Germany's Bundesliga. 'After Mexico, people thought Japanese football was getting better,' he explained. 'Some players then had offers and could have gone abroad. But they stayed on for the sake of Japanese football. By the time I reached my peak, Japan couldn't make it to the Olympics or the World Cup and the JSL was not that popular. I couldn't do it all on my own.' After a slow start, the Germans were surprised at the speed and ability of the arrival from the East, and when Köln did the double in his first year, newspapers ran features on '*der gelbe Blitz*' – the 'yellow lightning'. In Japan the media largely ignored him, a curiosity in a minor sport. 'No German replica shirts were sold because of me,' he said. 'It was not big news in Japan, and my games were only rarely on TV. No one was interested.'

During his time in West Germany, Okudera tried to contribute to Japanese football on his trips home. But every time he made a suggestion for how a team could improve, the response was always negative. Whenever he asked why, they always replied: 'Because Japan is different.' In 1986, after nine seasons in the Bundesliga, playing for Hertha Berlin after Köln, and finally Werder Bremen, he returned to Japan to play out the rest of his career. But he found he had learnt to play a different game. He ran where he expected to receive a pass, but it never came. In terms of the flow and build-up of a football game, 'they were thinking different things from me,' he said later. 'And when I asked them to do something, they said, "We can't do that."' At the time, he told an interviewer: 'To be honest, I feel Japanese football is shut up inside a shell.'

A couple of JSL teams did start taking football more seriously. Yomiuri Club, owned by the *Yomiuri* newspaper, took on a 21-year-old Japanese-Brazilian called Jorge Yonashiro. Despite having never played more than kick-around football in Brazil, he was still good enough for Yomiuri's first team. And Nissan FC decided to strengthen its squad in 1987 with two Brazilians. One, Wagner Lopes, was a gangly eighteen–year–old who wanted to escape his low standard of living at home and see the world. The other was Oscar, a tall defender who had represented his country sixty times, including the 1978, 1982 and 1986 World Cup campaigns, and wanted to play out the final two years of his career in Japan. In Brazil Oscar could not go outside without being mobbed by fans, who called out to him '*Capitão! Capitão!*' because he had captained both Brazil and Sao Paulo FC. In the days before the Brazilians' first game in Japan, Lopes scoured the papers for stories building up to his and the veteran's debut appearances. There were none. When the players walked out on the pitch for the game, the stadium was almost empty, and Oscar said to Lopes: 'Maybe there isn't a match today.' Eventually around 2,000 spectators drifted in after work. The standard of play was equally shocking to the Brazilians. When one team's defenders got the ball, they didn't pass it around the midfield to try to build up an attack; they booted it up the pitch in the hope of getting a lucky break. 'The system was set at 4-4-2, but it only stayed that way till kick-off,' Lopes remembered. 'After the start, the players just swarmed around the ball. It was like children's football.'

By the mid-1980s, the generation of footballers that had

played in the Olympic teams of the 1960s worried the game was all but dead. Before the 1984 Los Angeles Olympics, for example, expectations rose for a young attacking team built up by a coach who had taken over in 1981. They beat Brazilian powerhouse Sao Paulo Corinthians in two out of three practice matches in January 1984. And for the final Asian qualifying round in Singapore in April, all their opponents looked beatable: Malaysia, Iraq, Qatar and Thailand. But Japan lost its first match to a weak Thai side 5–2. Then the players lost their confidence and went down 2–1 in the remaining three games.

A year later, Japan needed to win a two-match series with Asia's footballing kings South Korea to qualify for the Mexico World Cup. In the previous meeting Japan had beaten the Koreans for the first time in five years, and in the first game at Tokyo's National Stadium a confident Japan side attacked furiously from the kick-off. Even the defenders joined in the assault on the Korean goal, and for the first time at a Japanese football match an optimistic crowd of 62,000 began chanting: 'Ni-ppon! (clap clap clap) Ni-ppon! (clap clap clap)'. But after twenty-five minutes the Japanese had yet to score. And, by now, they were exhausted. The Koreans, still fresh after sitting back and soaking up the pressure, counter-attacked. On the half-hour they scored by knocking in a loose ball the Japanese goalkeeper had failed to clear. A few minutes before half time they added another. Though Japan pulled one goal back, South Korea won 2–1, and went on to win the return leg in Seoul 1–0. When the Koreans didn't simply overwhelm the Japanese, they could out-fox them. Japan had failed yet again. Since Mexico in 1968, ten coaches had struggled to improve the national team, but for twenty years they produced the same result: boring kick-and-run football that better organised teams could run rings around.

The solution was staring at them over the Sea of Japan. South Korea had formed a league with professional teams in 1983, and they consistently beat the Japanese. They would continue to qualify for the finals of every World Cup from 1986 onwards. Said Japanese national coach Takaji Mori after the twin defeats to South Korea: 'The Koreans have surpassed us in everything. I feel strongly that we too have to turn professional.'

Despite his frustrations on arriving back from Germany, Okudera did spark one important change. Though the JFA only recognised 'amateurs', Okudera had already crossed the line into professionalism. To accommodate him, the JFA set up a 'Special Licence Player System', and one other player, Kazushi Kimura of Nissan, who had been selected for an Asian 'Best Eleven', was also allowed to turn pro. Soon others wanted to do the same. Yomiuri Club tried to function like a European-style club, and had strengthened its side over the past decade with a number of Brazilians. Though several companies were against professionalism, opposition was softened by the recognition of some professional athletes at the 1984 Olympics. From the Seoul Olympics in 1988, this was scheduled to extend to football, making amateurism in top-level sport an anachronism. In any case, companies like Nissan and Yomiuri were already spending up to a billion yen (£5 million) a year on football, and it took a vivid imagination to see the players as amateurs. In 1987, the 'Special' was removed from the licence system, and more professionals were recognised.

By this time, the number of schoolchildren playing football outnumbered those playing baseball, which was the only team sport in Japan that was officially professional. What's more, Japan had become rich and fun-loving. Japanese manufacturers had cornered the world markets for video recorders, microchips and cars, and these exports had produced several decades of growth that outstripped North America and Europe. Japan's GDP was now over half that of the United States and three times the size of Britain's, and this success bred the idea that economically Japan could do no wrong. A new kind of wealth was created: the paper wealth of what became known as the bubble economy. Tokyo's stock exchange outstripped New York's in terms of market capitalisation. At its peak, the Nikkei average of leading stocks ballooned to nearly 40,000 yen. Regular folk who happened to own modest homes in Tokyo became overnight millionaires. The Japanese felt wildly rich. They sprinkled gold leaf in their champagne and on their sushi, and bought everything from foreign holidays to designer handbags. If the US could support four major professional sports leagues, surely Japan could manage another besides baseball.

When Kawabuchi became general secretary of the Japan Football Association in 1988, his reaction to the idea was characteristically blunt: 'That's just stupid, isn't it,' he said. Japanese football was too weak and too dull, and the league crowds were so small they were sad. How would re-labelling the game 'professional' make anyone start watching? And while improving the national team might appeal to the minority already interested in football, why should anyone else care? By the late 1980s, Japan's national self-esteem had inflated in step with the stock market to dizzying levels, and most Japanese would have no interest in such a modest aim as catching up with Chinese and South Korean football: they did not want to compete only with other Asians, or become moderately good at anything. To capture the interest of ordinary Japanese, a new professional league would need to possess the glamour and international stars on display in Europe. And it would have to spur the national team to a level where it could compete beyond the confines of Asia.

So, despite his reservations, in October 1989, Kawabuchi announced a plan for a professional league intended to revolutionise Japanese football. From the company football that Brazilians had compared to children's street games, the new league aimed to turn Japan into a regular World Cup qualifier – as well as the competition's first Asian host in 2002. Teams in the old JSL represented companies; for the new league, they would all have to change their names to the towns they played in, and run a network of youth teams designed to encourage young locals to participate. Kawabu-chi thought these might provide a springboard to sports

19

clubs like the *Sportschule* he had seen in Germany. He had grown up by the coast in an Osaka suburb, and spent his childhood fishing and swimming in the sea, and playing sumo and hide-and-seek in the grounds of Shinto shrines. In Duisburg he had thought about how much he would have enjoyed this kind of place too. 'Now everything in Japan is covered in concrete,' he lamented. 'Children sit in air-conditioned rooms and play TV games. Kids don't climb trees or get muddy like they used to.' His ideal was something like FC Barcelona, which was owned and run by thousands of local stakeholders and had teams of different levels in several sports under a football team that formed the main attraction. The JSL had attracted tiny crowds; the new teams would all have 15,000-seat stadiums with floodlights. A little ambitious? 'If things had carried on like before,' Kawabuchi said shortly after the J.League's launch, 'football in Japan would simply have disappeared. So I thought, why not take a chance?'

The conditions for joining the league demanded a lot of money. Most of the new hometowns would have to build new stadiums, and Kawabuchi warned owners of potential J.League teams to expect losses of about one billion yen (£5 million) a year for the first ten years. Flush with cash as Japan's biggest companies were at the end of the 1980s, they still needed a reason to throw their money at football teams.

They found one in a powerful combination of forces blowing through post-bubble-economy Japan. From the introduction of western sports to Japan in the nineteenth century, the Japanese had always treated them as more than just play. Meiji-era Japan had embarked on a national mission to catch up with the western industrialised powers and so avoid colonisation like other parts of Asia. In such circumstances simply playing seemed an unaffordable luxury, so educators made sure games acted as vehicles to nurture young men and women. Once the rules of western sports had been learned from western teachers, Japanese coaches grafted on traditional values – like the hierarchy, obedience and stoicism of the samurai era. Because of its overwhelming popularity, baseball was the most obvious vehicle for these ideals, and was often played as *seishin-yakyu* – spiritual baseball. This aimed to foster teamwork and mental and physical toughness, in a Japanese version of the rugby-and-rowing culture that developed empire-builders in British boarding schools. In gruelling training sessions, students were pummelled with balls from close range, after which they were told to say '*kayui*' – 'it itches' – rather than admit to actual pain. After throwing practice they hung from the branches of cherry trees to straighten their arms out.

Japan approached the years following its World War Two defeat with a similar determination to pick itself up and overtake the West. Professional baseball teams were, of course, outside the realm of education, and instead resembled the ideal Japanese business, with disciplined, tireless workers happy to follow orders from above. As a play-by-play game, coaches played a large part in baseball, signalling from the bench how each move was to proceed. Far more than in the American game, the head coach's decisions were perceived in Japan as the crucial factor in winning. During live transmissions, TV cameras hovered on the dugout so commentators could size up the boss's expression and speculate on his next move. When the Tokyo Giants won the Nihon Series play-offs nine times in a row – from 1965 to 1973, head coach Tetsuji Kawakami's method became widely known as '*kanri-yakyu*' – 'management baseball' – because his coaching and management techniques appeared to echo those of a successful corporate administrator. He understood the value of discipline in an organisation, made wise tactical decisions, and brought out the best in his underlings (the players). Kawakami's book '*Aku no kanrigaku*' – roughly translated as 'Bad-Assed Management Studies' – became a best-seller.

By the 1990s these values had outlasted their usefulness. Disciplined group workers, skilled at replicating and improving products invented elsewhere, had been effective while Japan was in catch-up mode. But now the Japanese realised they needed to think more freely and liberate their creative instincts to maintain their economic success. In football, each player had to decide what to do by himself. The coach could try to make himself heard from the bench, but as there were few natural breaks in the game, the decision-maker for each 'play' was whoever had the ball at that moment. The other twenty-one players, instead of standing where they were told, had to make snap decisions to run into space or cover a member of the opposition. There could be no better sport for 1990s Japan. 'The Japanese *salaryman* – lifelong corporate employee – likes projecting himself onto sports, and until recently this meant nothing but baseball,' summed up Fusaho Awata, author of several books on Japan's leisure industry. 'But now, as the times are changing, it is no longer acceptable to equate companies with baseball-style management. Companies now need more people like top footballers, who can grasp the overall picture, make instant judgements and change instantly from defence to attack.'

Of course these perceptions were partly the result of the Japanese tendency to make games perform some symbolic task. But if that was how people thought, then Japan's boardrooms – always sensitive to image and alert to the spirit of the times – would pay attention. They were also under pressure to be better corporate citizens, and give back to society rather than just generate bigger profits. Kiichi Miyazawa, prime minister from 1991 to 1993, declared that Japan's mission after achieving economic greatness was to become a 'lifestyle superpower'. Football was the perfect vehicle for corporations to demonstrate both their largesse and their embrace of the creative workplace.

Steel producer Sumitomo Metals, for example, was running an image-building TV commercial featuring a celebrity who asked simply: 'Are you flexible?' The company was also preparing a 'Year 2000 Vision' of its future, calling for ways to brighten up the lives of its employees and their families, and contribute something to Kashima, location of the company's main plant. Kashima was a small industrial town fifty miles up the Pacific coast from Tokyo, and its 60,000 residents had little to do after work besides rent videos, sing *karaoke* and play *pachinko*, a kind of vertical pinball. Looking for ways to liven up Kashima, a band of citizens formed a 'Make Kashima More Fun Discussion Group'. The group thought of using the shrine as a basis for a historical theme park, or developing a marine resort by the sea. But both would take time and money.

Then Sumitomo Metals came up with a proposal. The company's football team was based in Kashima, and though it was only in the second division of the Japan Soccer League, why not make the necessary investment to strengthen the squad and enter the J.League? For Sumitomo Metals, the annual one billion yen (£5 million) in running costs would be small change compared to the 30 or 40 billion a year it invested in each of its steel plants. For Kashima, a J.League team would be a perfect source of entertainment and pride for the townspeople. Kawabuchi said that for such a small town starting with just a second division team it was '99.9999 per cent impossible to join' the J.League unless it built a brand-new stadium with a 15,000 capacity. So the local council joined forces with three neighbouring towns, put up 8.4 billion yen (£50 million), and constructed Japan's first roofed stadium made solely for football.

The J.League hit a window of opportunity. A few years earlier, when Japanese businesses were satisfied with their direction, football might not have sparked any interest. In the mid-1990s, the recession-hit owners of the company teams would not have spared the extra cash. But in 1990, in spite of the tough conditions laid down by the J.League, twenty of the twenty-eight teams in the JSL's top two divisions applied to join. Ten of these were accepted, and they all renamed themselves, adding exotic foreign monikers to their town names. Nissan FC became Yokohama

Marinos, using the Spanish word for sailor, because Yokohama was a port. Yomiuri Football Club called its first team 'Verdy' from *verde*, Portuguese for green, because they played in green and had several Brazilian players. 'Gamba Osaka' came from the Italian word for leg, which also sounded like the way Osakans said *ganbaru*, a Japanese word for 'try hard'. And Sumitomo Metals FC became Kashima Antlers, as Kashima literally meant 'Deer Island'.

This willingness to invest up-front was a dream come true for the J.League's architects. But it would count for nothing unless the Japanese started watching and spending money on football. Accompanied by representatives of the future member clubs, J.League officials took a tour of Europe in order to learn how to run them. In particular, they spent three days at Bayer Leverkusen in Germany, where they learnt about the wage structure and scouting. Japanese baseball teams paid annual salaries that were unaffected by a player's performance. Leverkusen officials told them about the three types of pay they used – basic salary, appearance fee and winning fee – which provide an incentive to play to win. The J.League adopted this system.

But the financing of the new league was complex. Kawabuchi had wanted to wean the nation off corporate sports, and was instinctively anti-commercial. His first blueprint for the league envisioned no league sponsors, like most European football Leagues. 'I thought it should be like England where they had never had this,' he said.

But to start with a bang, the league needed star players and publicity, requiring big outlays by the new teams. Again the timing was right. As well as catching businesses at their most generous, the J.League could draw on powerful new techniques to generate money from sport. The 1984 Los Angeles Olympics had been a milestone in sports marketing, developing a system that raised the value of the event to sponsors by limiting their numbers to thirty, with no more than one from each product sector. Enticed by this, sponsors paid more money to the Games' organisers. Then, to make the most of their expensive investments, the sponsors launched advertising campaigns and products featuring the Olympic logo – free publicity for the Olympics. The LA Olympics were the first ever to make a profit, and US sports leagues began to use similar methods to raise their brand profiles and earn royalties at the same time.

Until this point, few European clubs had put much effort into sports marketing, and most were content to sell fans scarves and T-shirts. So while the club system and wage structure came from Europe, the J.League looked to the US to learn sports marketing, and Kawabuchi (and about twenty other members of the J.League Preparation Committee) went on a study tour. A group of National Football League officials taught them how to manage licensed goods and the rights for photos and TV. They went to the Super Bowl in the Rose Bowl in Pasadena, California, where Super Bowl banners hung in the streets, and each seat was provided with a 'Super Bowl XXVII' cushion and a bag of merchandise such as player cards. 'We were really impressed with the Super Bowl merchandizing,' remembered Kazuki Sasaki, who became J.League general secretary. 'We thought, "This is how you give fans proper service." This showed us how to turn a sports contest into an event, and how to market a sport.'

They learned how the NBA and NFL endorsed products, ran shops to sell them from, engaged league and individual team sponsors, and charged handsomely for broadcast rights. Kawabuchi soon dropped his concerns about commercialism. And when in 1992 England's top football division was renamed the Barclays Premier League, Kawabuchi decided to do the same for the J.League. The first half of the season became the Suntory Series, after a drinks maker, and the second the Nicos Series, after a credit card company. 'We needed the money,' he explained.

Marketing men also helped with the other big task: to convince the public that the J.League was a world apart from the dull old football of the JSL. Mizuno, Japan's largest maker of sports goods, was keen to expand beyond its core lines of golf and baseball goods, and its football representative Junichi Ishikawa visited the J.League Preparation Committee to angle for a contract. 'The best way to show that [football] has changed since the JSL is to have all-new uniforms with a changed image,' he told them. 'If we leave this to the individual teams, they will lack a co-ordinated image and be a muddle.' Persuaded, the committee let the teams choose their own colours (though it rejected some first choices because too many asked for blue), then commissioned Mizuno to design co-ordinated strips. Instead of the simple designs used by most of the world's football teams, Mizuno splashed the shirts with bright colours in abstract shapes. The final line-up, displayed at a fashion parade in May 1992, looked like a dessert trolley. Yokohama Marinos had blue shirts streaked with red and white paintbrush strokes. Verdy Kawasaki had a green and white tie-dye look. Hiroshima Sanfrecce wore purple shirts spangled round the shoulders with orange, green and white polygons.

To handle the licensing business, the J.League engaged Sony Creative Products, a subsidiary of the consumer electronics giant. Sony Creative had been formed in 1978 to produce toys based on *Sesame Street* characters for the Japanese market. It had since branched out into other themes, including *Thomas the Tank Engine*. Sony Creative did the same for the J.League. Designers scoured foreign sports magazines to see the team emblems and mascots used in the NFL, NBA and European football leagues. Then they came up with characters and logo marks that looked like animated cartoons. Yokohama Marinos were given a seagull dressed up in sailor's uniform. Local rivals Yokohama Flügels were owned by an airline and named after the German word for 'wing'; they got an aeroplane wearing a hat, as well as a Snoopy-type dog wearing a cape called *Tobimaru-kun* – Flying Boy. And, no prizes for guessing it, Kashima Antlers got a deer.

Completing the fresh, international image, the new teams brought in a dazzling list of foreign stars. In the 1970s, when the North American Soccer League was attempting to bring football to the USA, the Americans had tried the same tack, and brought in international stars such as Pele, Franz Beckenbauer and Johan Neeskens. But all played for the same team, New York Cosmos. Moreover, the imported foreigners obscured local players who might one day become role models to the young. After a few years the league shut down. Learning from the Americans' mistakes, the J.League limited the number of foreigners playing to three per team – enough to lay on star quality for the fans and show how the game is really played, but not so many as to prevent the rise of home-grown heroes who might become an even greater attraction.

Each team had its star. Zico, the 'white Pele' who had played for Brazil at three World Cups, signed for Kashima Antlers. He had retired two years previously, but liked the idea of promoting football in Japan, and was attracted by Kashima's ambition to create a new town identity through the game. England's Gary Lineker, top scorer in the 1986 Mexico World Cup, went to Nagoya Grampus Eight. Pierre Littbarski, the pixy-like midfielder who had won the 1990 World Cup with West Germany, joined JEF United Ichihara. Former Argentine international Ramon Diaz joined Yokohama Marinos, and Brazil's Edu signed for Yokohama Flügels. Before it had even started, the J.League was a Who's Who of recent World Cup history.

The hometown idea, the marketing gimmicks, the stars – all were so novel that a year before its start, the J.League became a major news story. When Kawabuchi announced that the league would take the radical step of counting ticket stubs to announce true attendance figures, the major dailies ran news analysis pieces questioning the established baseball practice of always announcing the same inflated round number of spectators to try and convince people their team was a good draw. (The standard attendance figures claimed by several teams were higher than their ballparks' capacity. 'The announced figure is just a long-standing business tradition,' one fire-prevention agent was quoted as saying. 'As long as the number of people doesn't actually exceed the capacity, it has nothing to do with us.') Four hundred and forty media people swarmed to the 1992 preview of uniforms and accessories, getting the league featured on the national evening news and in newspapers and magazines. When several hundred people stood in line for the opening of the first official J.League shop – named 'CATEGORY-1' after the best seats in European football stadiums – this was another news story. One hundred of these shops plus another hundred department-store booths opened before the league even began. The J.League spent about 500 million yen (£3 million) on publicity from 1991 to 1993, but in the three months before it kicked off, media reports produced the equivalent of 200 or 300 million-yen (around £2 million) worth of commercials every day. Kawabuchi estimated this added up to 10 or 20 billion yen (up to £100 million) worth of publicity. What's more, just like at the LA Olympics, official sponsors produced advertisements generating even more publicity. Uniform supplier Mizuno arranged for Japan's top TV comedy duo to do a TV commercial in which they implored: 'Hurry up and start, J.League!'

When tickets went on sale for the opening match, 306,269 people applied. On 15 May 1993, over 50,000 of these crammed into the National Stadium, and watched a pop concert followed by a display of smoke bombs, coloured lights and fireworks. Football? It was more like rock and roll. Then Verdy Kawasaki and Yokohama Marinos played the J.League's first game. The metamorphosis of Japanese football was complete. Empty, run-down stadiums with brown grass, crude end-to-end punts and players who were company staff – that was frumpy Old Football. New Football had pastel uniforms, theme toys, Zico and Lineker, and stadiums with floodlights and moist green turf.

CHAPTER TWO

Stars

The stars needed to launch the J.League would be mostly at the ends of their careers, seeking a new challenge and willing to pass on experience gained from World Cups and Europe and South America's top leagues. They were also expected to act as role models, and display what Japanese clubs considered the correct bearing and conduct for a professional footballer. Though Japan was loosening up in the 1990s – formality and work had become a drag; sex and vacations were fun – there were still a few rules that were unbreakable. One of these was – no drugs. Diego Maradonna was popular in Japan and just the right age to put in a stint in the J.League. He had made some Japanese TV commercials, and was often rumoured to be on the way to play there. But after he tested positive for banned substances in 1991, no Japanese club would touch him. He was even forbidden from entering the country in 1994 for a friendly tournament, prompting the whole Argentina team to stay away.

Japan was also looking for attacking players more than defenders. Strikers were higher profile, and their main ability, setting up and scoring goals, was more easily appreciated by football novices than the stopping and subtle positioning of defensive players. In the words of Nagoya Grampus Eight general manager Narumi Nishigaki, when acquiring a foreign star to launch his new team, 'We had two aims. One was to acquire a player who could score goals, and the other was to form a team that played fairly.'

Gary Lineker was the perfect candidate. Approaching retirement, he was one of the world's top goalmouth predators, had never been yellow-carded, and came from a country that to most Japanese still represented tea-and-cake gentility. Nishigaki explained to him the idea behind the J.League, and after three months of negotiations they had a deal reported to be the biggest for any player in the league, with estimates ranging between 450 million and 700 million yen (around £2.5 million and £4 million) for a two-year contract. 'Gary Lineker had been the Golden Boot winner in the 1986 World Cup, and we thought his scoring ability would lead the team to victory,' Nishigaki said at the time. 'He has a sunny personality and is an intelligent sportsman. He speaks very logically and I think the Japanese people will all welcome this kind of person.'

From the moment Lineker arrived in Japan, everything went beautifully. Visiting Nagoya for the first time over four days in August 1992, nine months before the start of the J.League, he charmed and joked his way through jet lag and a tough schedule, greeting a press conference in Japanese and delighting his hosts and reporters with his wry sense of humour. It was very humid, and around 33 degrees, but because this was Japan, everyone wore a suit and tie. No matter. It was a lovely day, said Lineker, 'just right for swimming. But I don't know about running around at three in the afternoon!' Shown how to operate a computer in the Toyota showroom, he quipped: 'Will this help me score goals?'

When he went to the training ground, he was for the first time in his life applauded by his future teammates. The team stood in a big circle and Lineker was introduced to them one by one like a visiting dignitary, many of them so in awe of him that they seemed anxious about even shaking his hand. Team captain Shigeo Sawairi said: 'We looked at him like fans would. All the players were really pleased about the simple fact that Gary Lineker was on our team.' Sawairi liked Lineker's looks too: 'I thought Gary was like a fashion model. I had had an image of British players as being very tough and strong. But he didn't look like this. He wasn't that tall, not that much taller than the Japanese players. I even doubted that he could be a top-class player.'

The congenial mood continued when Linker returned in

1993 to prepare for the start of the league. First there was gratitude that he had come to Japan even though his baby son George had leukaemia and would need regular specialist treatment. Then Lineker threw himself into diplomatic activities with aplomb. He accompanied the team on a visit to a Shinto shrine in Nagoya, where the priest bestowed on them the luck of the gods, and girls in bright costumes performed a traditional dance. 'It was great,' he said. 'I didn't understand what was going on, but it was very attractive.' Following another Japanese tradition for celebrities, he was made 'police chief' for a day to promote public safety. Wearing a blue policeman's uniform, finished off with white cap, white belt, white epaulettes and a red rose, he toured the precinct around the Grampus stadium for two hours. Children lined the route waving Japanese and British flags. 'I'm really surprised,' he joked. 'I've only been in Japan two months, and I'm already police chief!' There was a pause for translation followed by more laughter, the kind of relieved group laughter heard in Japan when everything is going smoothly.

But Lineker's right big toe had been troubling him, and after his first visit to Nagoya he underwent an operation. He then trained at his old club Tottenham Hotspur to recover from this, while fitting in radio and TV work as well as lessons in Japanese and golf. Arriving in Nagoya he was overweight and had not played a professional game for seven months. Grampus's first J.League game was against Kashima Antlers, and was billed in the press as Lineker versus Zico, who was the Antlers' star. It was no contest. Lineker saw little of the ball. Zico scored a hat trick, and the Antlers won 5–0. Though they went on to beat Urawa Reds and Yokohama Marinos in their next two games, Lineker did not score, and reporters started asking him at post-match press conferences when he would consider getting his first goal.

Part of the problem was that, unlike Zico, Lineker was a pure striker rather than a game maker – he even joked himself that all his career goals had been goal hangs. He needed the rest of the team to create chances for him, but they didn't know how. They were also attempting a short passing game that he wasn't used to, and the easy smile that had so endeared him to his hosts soon began to fade as he ran round the pitch waiting for service that never came.

While Lineker failed to score at one end of the pitch, the Grampus defence was a sieve. They let in thirty-eight goals in the eighteen games of the 1993 first-stage championship, the worst defensive record in the league, and came ninth out of ten. 'They were quite gung-ho,' said Lineker later. 'It was 4–4–2, but the two full backs played as wingers. I tried to get one to always tuck back. I gave advice, but I was always wondering how it was translated. [Manager Hiraki] was a lovely guy, and he loved his football. But he didn't have that much experience.'

Another problem was the Nagoya home pitch, which turned into mud and puddles in the late spring rains. A year or so later, Yugoslav Dragan Stojkovic famously celebrated its awfulness by keeping the ball up while running at full speed for fifteen metres, entertaining fans while making the point that the ball simply wouldn't travel along the surface. Lineker, however, had no such fun, and perhaps aggravated by the conditions, his toe's condition worsened. He was often substituted in pain or left out of the side, and in October he stopped playing altogether. He visited a specialist in Chicago, had another operation, and spent the next eight months rehabilitating. Grampus came eighth in the second stage, and manager Hiraki resigned.

Back in the days when the country overflowed with money, the Japanese used to play a game with (white) foreigners that involved treating them better than they needed to, and then resenting the foreigner who did not appreciate the responsibilities this entailed. The beneficiaries ranged from overpaid English conversation teachers to expatriates working in finance, and also extended to sport. Bashing the overpaid foreigner had been a favourite pastime of baseball pundits, when US major leaguers came to Japan to breeze through their retirement years, picking up huge paycheques in return for putting in too little effort in what they considered an inferior league. Combined with the money they were getting, their perceived lack of effort made it look as if they were taking Japan lightly – treating the country without the respect it demanded.

After his honeymoon period with the Japanese media, it might have been Lineker's turn for this kind of attention. Grampus had indeed been naïve to think that simply planting a top striker at the head of the team would somehow yield goals. But they had also spent lots of money on the J.League's most glamorous, expensive star, who had then spent most of his time recovering from a toe injury, and only scored four goals. One newspaper, the *Sankei Sports*, accompanied Lineker's eventual retirement announcement with its calculation of his yen-per-goal rate in Japan: 175 million, or about £1 million per strike, counting just the league. Another is supposed to have labelled him 'Britain's most faulty export' – damning because of the country's then-poor reputation for manufactured goods.

But these were early days for Japanese football, and there was relatively little media flak directed his way. The fans, too, were still innocent enough to think that insulting or complaining about players was inappropriate behaviour. 'I didn't like Lineker,' said Masatoshi Yoshida, one of the Grampus supporters' group leaders. 'He didn't do his job. But we didn't know then how to get angry at football matches. We didn't know about hurling abuse at players.'

Yet for many, perhaps most, Grampus fans the issue never arose. Their love for Gary was blind. One young fan, Hisashi Komoto, had fallen for him because of the equaliser he scored against West Germany in the 1990 World Cup semi-final. Though Komoto's home was in the suburbs outside Tokyo, he chose to go to a college near Nagoya just to be near Lineker. Later he even chose 'lineker@ . . . ' for his e-mail address. 'People like me felt bad for Lineker that he had come to Grampus,' he said. 'We thought Grampus was not good enough for him.'

Lineker himself didn't put it that rudely. 'It was frustrating at times,' he said. 'But I was realistic about my ambitions on the pitch. When I first signed, it was not just to play, but also to promote the game in that country. I wasn't really there for my footballing skills.' And for most fans that was enough. At his final match, one young man said, 'I became a fan because Lineker joined Grampus. I know he's leaving today, but from now on I'm going to support them as my local team.'

Even the Lineker-doubters were moved by this final game. The last league match of the year, it had a carnival atmosphere, and Grampus fans agreed to make their support for the game Lineker-only. Some wore Tottenham hats, while others waved Union Jacks. 'We love Gary,' proclaimed one banner. Predictably, after a poor first half performance he was substituted early in the second half, but the emotion – over the greatest sports star ever to live in Nagoya, who had been beset by troubles and never shone, and who was now leaving – was overwhelming. Tadakatsu Nishi, another supporter, summed up the feeling: 'He had hardly played, but when he did play we always thought something good might happen. Then, after the matches he did play I always felt disappointed. But at the final match, I began to remember all the things he and Grampus had gone through. I had felt cynical earlier in the year when the TV news reported "Lineker training again", after he'd been out injured all that time. But now I decided I should have been warmer towards him and supported him more. I thought about the effort he had made towards his come-back. I remembered how his son had been ill, and that he had come to Nagoya in spite of this. I had been complaining constantly about him, but now I thought that in just a few minutes, the great Gary Lineker would retire. And I cried. Everyone cried.'

At first, most J.League fans were happy just to bathe in the reflected glory of the foreign stars. When Italia 90 golden boot winner Salvatore Schillaci joined Jubilo Iwata in 1994, he scored one goal and set up the other in a 2–0 victory in his first match, against the previous year's champions Verdy Kawasaki. In a post-match interview with the *Gazzetta dello Sport* he said: 'Instead of playing my best, I tried to put on a show to please the fans. In spite of that, the Japanese players still couldn't keep up with my dribbling. It's much less tiring than the Serie A, but it was quite mentally tiring having to fit in with the low level of the game.'

This was, of course, picked up by the Japanese sports press, which sometimes appeared to take masochistic pleasure in the spectacle of foreigners being rude about Japan. There was a suspicion that most of the foreign imports, even if they were not so blatant, shared this patronising view of the game in Japan. But there was one significant exception – the great Zico. Here was a player that combined star quality with a determination to improve the Japanese game. Zico was everything Japanese football wanted from a foreign player.

Zico had retired in 1989 after a career in which he was recognised as one of the best footballers ever. He had played eighty-nine times for Brazil and scored sixty-eight goals, a tally second only to Pele. He was South American player of the year in 1977 and 1982, and world player of the year in 1983. In 1981 he led his Rio de Janeiro club Flamengo to victory in the Copa Libertadores, the South American club championship, and then to a 3–0 victory over Liverpool to win the European-South American Intercontinental Club Championship, a game in which he was chosen Most Valuable Player. But despite playing in three World Cups – 1978, 1982 and 1986 – and being chosen as player of the tournament in the middle one of these, Zico never played for a Brazilian World Cup winning team. He never even made it to a semi-final. Never winning the World Cup was his biggest regret, he wrote later: 'Because of this I will always be another player who never became number one.'

Whatever his reasons, Zico found it hard to quit football. Chosen to become Brazil's first sports minister in March

1990, he soon tired of politics and living in the capital, Brasilia. So when a Japanese club approached to ask if he would play for them, he was interested. Two years before the start of the J.League, the Sumitomo Metals football team had still not changed into the Kashima Antlers, and it seemed an unlikely place for one of the greatest players in the history of the game. They were not even in the top flight of the Japan Soccer League, meaning that until the J.League started, Zico would be playing in the second division of a minor football country. But the move had some logic. Zico had fond memories of trips to Japan in his playing days. Tokyo had been the scene for his Intercontinental Cup triumph against Liverpool. And in 1989 he had played in a match featuring former World Cup stars, and taught a football class over two days in Saitama, a prefecture north of the capital. Though he had heard football was not that popular in Japan, over a thousand children had turned up on both days. They listened to his every word, watched his every move, and kept shouting 'Zico-san! Zico-san!' – 'Mr Zico!' in their enthusiasm. Zico had always planned to open football schools after retiring as a player, and liked the idea of including Japanese children in the plan. So when his agent told him about the enquiry from Japan and the new professional league planned there, Zico jumped at the chance.

When Zico joined the Sumitomo Metals football team in 1991, reporters guessed he received a $1 million signing fee and a salary of $500,000 a year for three years – which came to a total of about half the upper estimates for Lineker's bill. Conditions were typical for a smaller Japanese company football team. The club had no practice ground of its own, so the squad practised on earth pitches in different locations each day. The ball bobbled along the irregular surface, and falling over meant getting a mouthful of dirt. The players had to wash their training gear themselves, and use showers inside the Sumitomo Metals plant. On match days, they painted the lines on the pitch themselves. More than professional football, it felt like a Sunday morning kick-around. When the season started, opponents in the JSL second division asked Zico before the game for autographs and souvenir photographs with him.

After the J.League began and the club became the Antlers, Zico started a drive to turn it into a professional organisation. The night before matches, he stayed in the club dormitory with the players and checked they didn't go out drinking. He lectured them on how to treat fans that came to watch training – always take time to sign autographs, shake hands and take pictures. 'Don't forget that you are fighting along with the fans,' he told them. Another time he warned players that, 'Your responsibility has become much heavier. We have to hold up the name, not just of the Antlers, but of Kashima.' On one occasion, shocked to see muddy football boots lying around the dressing room, he picked one up and asked: 'Whose is this boot?' The boots were all supplied by a sponsor, and nobody knew. As a boy, Zico had borrowed other peoples' boots until a friend of his father's bought him some for his test to join Flamengo, and they held a talismanic significance for him. He demanded the players clear up the boots, then took his own pair out of their bag, and began polishing them to demonstrate the care and respect they deserved.

The challenges on the field were even greater. When Zico first arrived, few players could control the ball properly or knew which part of the field to stand on. More than skill and tactics however, the biggest problem was attitude. They didn't seem to care much about winning. Worse, they sometimes joked around in the dressing room after losing. Zico hollered at Japanese players he caught laughing after defeats, and lectured Brazilians he had brought in on their responsibilities – always in front of the other players, to demonstrate his lack of bias. Berating Santos for not trying hard enough, he said: 'What was that last piece of play? If you did that kind of thing in Brazil, you would be booed. If you're just here to earn money, you're making a big mistake. You must not disrespect Japan.'

By the time the J.League started, the combination of

Brazilian players and Zico's education had turned the Antlers into one of Japan's top teams. They won the first-stage championship with thirteen wins out of eighteen (the league had no points system at first, and just counted wins). The reason, according to Zico, was that 'they fought with a more professional spirit than other teams.'

So great was Zico's desire for achievement that it created trouble. Though formally at Kashima as a player, he thought he had been brought there to help develop the club. So even when he was sidelined by the knee injuries and muscle pulls that afflicted his forty-year-old body, he still turned up for training every day to instruct the players. This meant the official team manager was squeezed out of his role. At fifty-five years old, Masakatsu Miyamoto came from the era of corporate amateurs, and shortly after the Antlers won the first-stage championship Zico told reporters that he and Miyamoto had never had any real communication. Moreover, Zico added, 'I think of myself as the manager. I am the one who has pulled the team along.' The quote was plastered over the tabloids the next day: 'Zico – I am the manager!'

His authoritarian didactic style of management went one step further when he started getting cranky with his interpreter Kunihiro Suzuki, who he worried was acting as a cushion for his anger, softening his admonitions into gentler, more Japanese tones. So Zico made his interpreter shout in the same harsh tone. 'Before I educated the players, I had to educate the interpreter,' he said. Even this education caused aggravation, and Suzuki once threatened to resign because of Zico's rough tone. 'You were my idol,' Suzuki complained. 'It's painful having someone who was your idol getting angry at you.'

Zico said the pressure he felt came from his feelings of responsibility to the players: lose and some would be fired when the time came to renew contracts. And he began to think that opposition teams were not all that was preventing the Antlers from winning. While the J.League got so much right at first, the referees were still from the old days of corporate-amateur sport, when results did not affect the financial success and therefore payroll of a team, and there were only a handful of spectators at most games. Later the league invited foreign referees, both to officiate and give lectures to Japanese referees. But in 1993, they were firmly amateur, and their decisions were often questionable.

In the 1993 Nabisco (League) Cup, the Antlers were knocked out in the group stage of the competition on goal difference, after the Brazilian Alcindo had a goal disallowed one minute before the end of their last game against Hiratsuka Bellmare. Videos later showed he had not been offside. Alcindo also complained that four or five goals had been 'stolen' from him by referees in the first stage through faulty offside calls and failures to award penalties after tackles from behind in the box. He was suspended for four matches after a game against Yokohama Marinos after he first threw the ball at the referee, and later burst into his dressing room to continue protesting.

Some players managed to live with the decisions. Gary Lineker, true to his reputation, maintained excellent discipline. In the first match between Antlers and Grampus in 1993, Lineker put the ball in the left-hand corner of the net with a right-foot shot, but the linesman flagged for offside and the goal was disallowed. Lineker just sat on the ground and held his head in his hands. 'That was not offside,' he said later, 'but in a later match I may get a goal allowed even though it is offside. You can't complain to the referee.'

Lineker's composure had, of course, been a big factor in bringing him to Japan. But if Japanese football was going to benefit from foreign players, it also needed to be challenged by brusquer characters. Zico was not as controlled as Lineker, and thought his protests were a contribution to the development of the J.League. 'If I say things about the refereeing,' he told one reporter, 'it is because I think that, as well as players, referees have to make progress too.'

Yokohama Flügels manager Shu Kamo, who had spent years managing Nissan's team in the JSL, probably came closest to the truth about referees when he said: 'When I was at Nissan, foreign players always said that though Japanese referees were no good, they were the fairest in the world. If one call goes against you, another one will go for you.' But Zico was convinced the referees were biased, even if unconsciously, in favour of Kawasaki Verdy, Antlers' main rivals for the championship. As Yomiuri Club, Verdy had been one of the top JSL teams, and their top players now formed the backbone of the Japan national team, including captain Tetsuji Hashiratani, star striker Kazuyoshi Miura, and Ruy Ramos, a popular former-Brazilian who had taken Japanese nationality. While the Antlers were upstarts from the countryside and seen simply as Zico's team, Verdy were the pride of Japanese football.

When Verdy won the second-stage championship in 1993, setting up a play-off with first-stage champions the Antlers, Zico urged the J.League to invite an overseas referee to officiate the championship matches. He was also angry that both legs in the play-off were scheduled for Tokyo's National Stadium. Though this was supposed to be neutral ground, Verdy had played a total of ten league games there in 1993, making it a home from home for them.

Zico was out injured for the first leg, and Verdy won 2–0. In the second leg, the Antlers were leading 1–0 at halftime after Alcindo volleyed a goal in the thirty-eighth minute. One more goal would clinch a draw. After thirteen minutes of the second half, Verdy midfielder Paulo brought down Alcindo from behind in the Verdy penalty area, but the referee Shizuo Takada did nothing. With ten minutes remaining and the score still 1–0 to the Antlers, Paulo tangled with Antlers defender Eiji Gaya in the penalty area, and Paulo fell over dramatically. The referee blew the whistle immediately for a penalty. After noisy protests from Santos and Alcindo, the ball was placed on the spot.

It was all too much for Zico. He had come out of retirement, played in the second division of Japan's corporate amateur league, then built up the Antlers to one of Japan's best teams. The Antlers had lost two weeks previously to the Yokohama Flügels in the Emperor's Cup final, and Zico was staking everything on the J.League championship. But now, just before the moment that would justify all this effort, a referee was about to take it away. Zico walked up to the ball. He bent over it, as if to check it was properly on the spot – and spat.

He had already received one yellow card, and Takada gave him his second of the match. It was only the fifth time he had been sent off in a twenty-five-year career that had been marked by elegance both in play and manners. This time, as he left the field, he applauded the referee. Miura converted the penalty without difficulty to tie the match at 1–1. That was also the final score, and Verdy won the first ever J.League championship.

Zico was suspended for four games: one for getting two yellow cards in a match; one for rough conduct; and two for insulting the referee. J.League chairman Kawabuchi produced the most damning condemnation of the incident, saying, 'It was as if he had spat at the J.League itself.' Dutchman Frans van Balkom, a coach with Verdy at the time, was more charitable and said later that Zico had simply cared too much.

Back in the dressing room after Zico was sent off, he told his interpreter how much losing the championship meant to him. 'Since I came to Japan, I have always put my heart and soul into it. I didn't want to be another foreign player who didn't do enough, and I did not let up once.' His voice was calm, and tears were visible in his eyes. Later, when his teammates returned from the awards ceremony, Zico told them: 'Everybody. Today we lost. But I don't want you to think about having lost. We didn't lose because your power was not enough. You are all champions. So let's be proud as champions. The Antlers era has started.'

No one had expected the Antlers to go so far – and they had at least won the first-stage championship. Few had heard of Kashima before, but now people across Japan knew the town as the home of the Antlers. It was even known in Brazil as the place Zico played. There was little of note in

Kashima, but the Antlers built some of the best football club facilities in the country – a clubhouse with a shop selling sports gear and accessories, and a restaurant with views of the training ground, which fans could use freely. Instead of earth pitches, there were three grass practice grounds with floodlights, a weight-training room and meeting rooms. In 1990/91, the season before Zico arrived, Sumitomo Metals had a total attendance for the season of 16,330, or 540 per match. In 1993, a total of 252,291 spectators watched Antlers' home games, an average of 14,016.

The following season Zico played seven games before hanging up his boots. But his work for the Antlers continued. He made sure the team had good Brazilian managers, flying in to take over himself for several months when the team went through a bad patch in 1999. The Antlers became one of Japan's two strongest clubs, and won the J.League championship three times. In 2000, Toninho Cerezo, a member alongside Zico of Brazil's 1982 midfield 'Golden Quartet', led the Antlers to the first treble in the J.League, winning the league championship, the Emperor's Cup and the Nabisco (League) Cup. To honour his contributions, the club erected a bronze statue of Zico outside the stadium.

Young Japanese could admire the foreign stars who played in the J.League, but they were always somehow out of reach. There was, however, one player any Japanese boy could dream of becoming: Kazuyoshi 'Kazu' Miura.

Kazu first stepped on the road to stardom because he was no good at football. He was born in Shizuoka, a medium-sized city on the Pacific coast, roughly a third of the way from Tokyo to Osaka. Shizuoka and the surrounding prefecture was the most football-crazy place in Japan. Long before the game had become popular in other regions, Tetsuji Hotta, a teacher in the town of Shimizu, began to tutor coaches at the town's junior schools in order to get children playing from a young age. Shimizu started Japan's first junior school league in 1967, and football soon became popular in the surrounding area. In the 1970s, Shizuoka schools won or were runners-up in the national high school championship six times. By 1980, when Kazu was growing up, 800 local teams and 28,000 players had registered with the prefecture football association. In the J.League era, about 15 per cent of Japan's professional footballers came from there, a place that accounted for just 3.8 million of the country's 120 million population.

Even more than most Shizuoka boys, Kazu grew up surrounded by football. His father was an official in the Shizuoka Football Association, and his uncle Yoshiro ran a football shop as well as a boys' team. The star of that team was Kazu's elder brother Yasutoshi. Yasu could run freely with the ball at his feet, touching it on every stride. He scored goals frequently, after which Uncle Yoshiro would clench his fist and shout: 'That's good, Yasu! Just keep them coming like that!' But Kazu was small for his age, slow, and not very well coordinated. He often lost interest mid-game, and his uncle berated him for standing around and not trying. Even when he did make an effort, the results didn't come easily. In one game, Kazu tried to cross the ball while running, but lost balance, missed the ball and fell over. His uncle took him out of the game, kicked him, and ordered him to run round the ground for the rest of the match.

This treatment eventually had its desired effect. Kazu began to rise at six every morning, cycle to a nearby park, and practise juggling a ball for an hour before breakfast. Skill became an obsession, and whenever he had other free time he practised dribbling and juggling. By the time he was eleven, he could keep the ball up hundreds of times with no difficulty. He could even turn a full circle while the ball was in the air, then continue juggling, and do the same with a forward roll. Team practice continued till after seven every evening, but Kazu and his brother then went off to the park, set up a pair of coke cans for a goal, and practised dribbling and shooting.

Kazu became quite skilful, but he was still small and

relatively slow. While Yasutoshi was chosen to play for prefecture youth teams, Kazu was left out. Then Uncle Yoshiro showed the boys some videos of the 1970, 1974 and 1978 World Cups. Till then, Japanese football's main influence had been Germany, and coaching had centred on teamwork and physical strength. The Brazilian team of the 1970 World Cup showed a different version of the game. Kazu was hooked, and started practising feints as he'd seen Rivelino do them, stepping over the ball to confuse defenders. Uncle Yoshiro told the boys: 'In the future, go to Brazil. If you go to Brazil, your body will learn real football.'

So in his final year of middle school, when his class filled in a form to say what they intended to do after leaving, Kazu filled in the column for first-choice high school with the word 'Brazil'. It took about a year. Kazu's father was now working in Sao Paulo, setting up a school for young Japanese players. He arranged for Kazu to enter a club in the same city called Juventus. Uncle Yoshiro told him that if he was going to Brazil, it wasn't enough just to practise there – he must become a professional footballer.

Kazu arrived in Brazil with $700 that his mother had given him. He began to live in the Juventus dormitory, sleeping on a bunk bed in a small, dirty room with five other boys. On his third night, he woke up scratching his stomach to find he had been bitten by fleas and ticks. For several nights he couldn't sleep because of the itching. Life was no more pleasant on the field. When the training season began in February, Kazu took part in a practice game in suburban Sao Paulo. First, his teammates wouldn't pass to him. Then, when he eventually got the ball, he tried dribbling, but was soon relieved of the ball. He heard a shout from the stands: '*Futebol japonês!*' – 'Japanese football!' Brazil had a large Japanese community, mostly descendants of immigrants who had sailed across the Pacific to escape the poverty of early twentieth-century Japan. They were generally good at business, and there was a prosperous area of Sao Paulo known as Little Tokyo. But Japanese-Brazilians had made little impact on Brazilian football. '*Futebol japonês*' meant playing as badly as only a Japanese could. Kazu's confidence was immediately shot and when his teammates too began to taunt him with '*Futebol japonês!*' it was all too much. After this, he was rarely asked to play, even in practice games, for his first six months. When he did, the treatment started again: 'Hey, *japonês*! Go to Little Tokyo and fry tempura!' 'How can you see the ball through those narrow eyes?'

Kazu improved his technique bit by bit through long hours of shooting and dribbling practice, and stayed at the training ground till after dark, doing two or three hundred sit-ups a day. To communicate better, he studied Portuguese twice a week at a school in Little Tokyo, and continued at night, lying on his bunk softly pronouncing words from a dictionary till he fell asleep with the book in his hand. His body became immune to the fleas, which no longer affected him.

But progress was slow. He was lonely, still didn't get on well with his teammates, and lost his enthusiasm. After two years and three months in Brazil, he was in a slump. He moved from Juventus to Quinze de Jau, a team in a small town about 300 kilometres from Sao Paulo, but still didn't improve much. Losing hope of ever making it, Kazu phoned his mother for the first time since going to Brazil, and told her he couldn't stand it any longer and was coming home. His mother told Uncle Yoshiro, who called Kazu back. 'What are you talking about!? You promised not to come back for five years. You do not want to come home – do you understand? You cannot come home!'

Kazu got on a bus to meet his father who was then living in Sao Paulo. But if he was looking for sympathy from his father, it wasn't forthcoming. 'Go back to Japan?' he shouted. 'OK, if you're that feeble, then get back to Japan!' He went red in the face and hit Kazu for the first time, a blow to the right cheek. 'OK,' Kazu told him. 'I'll go then.'

Before leaving Brazil for good, Kazu decided to do some

sightseeing, and took a train to Rio de Janeiro to see the famous Maracanã Stadium, site of the 1950 World Cup final and a Mecca for Brazilian football. He walked the back streets of Rio for a while, and sat down to rest in a small park. There he saw about twenty boys playing kick-around football. They were all about twelve years old, wore dirty, ripped shirts, and half of them had no shoes. One was trying to play even though he had only one leg, and was hopping around after the ball. Kazu was suddenly overwhelmed by how lucky he was, and began to feel angry with himself. He decided to give Brazil one more try.

After Rio, Kazu returned to Quinze de Jau with a fresh determination. He hit a streak of form. In a big amateur tournament, his team was 1–0 down when he was fouled in the penalty area. He converted the penalty, and heard shouts of 'Kazuuu! Kazuuu!' from the stands. It was the first time he had been called by his name rather than his nationality, '*Japonês*'. The next month, just before his nineteenth birthday, he was finally offered a professional contract with Santos.

That was not, however, the end of Kazu's struggle, and in six months at Santos he only played two matches. After the second of these, the newspapers rated his performance two out of ten, compared to a next-lowest mark of four for the other players on the field. They said he was slow and should go back to Japan. So for a couple of years he travelled to different parts of Brazil playing for clubs that would take him on. He turned out for a team called Matsubara, run by a Japanese-Brazilian of that name, in a rural part of Paraná state. It often took seven or eight hours to reach away matches by bus, and one trip took twenty-three hours each way. The players rolled up mats to use as pillows and slept on the floor of the bus, which shook from the potholes. Punctures were frequent, and every meal was at a motorway service station, where they served only grilled mutton – three or four times a day. The temperature at the ground was often 40 degrees centigrade.

After a brief period with Clube de Regattas Brasil, he was

given a contract by his old club, Quinze de Jau. In the Sao Paulo state championship, they played the mighty Corinthians in front of a packed house with lots of TV cameras lined up. Kazu was marked by former Brazil international Edilson. But he dribbled past him with a feint, passed the ball, and the next moment floated in the air to get on the end of the cross from the right. He headed into the left-hand corner. The goal gave Quinze a 3–2 victory over Corinthians, and the papers ran big stories the next day about '*O Karate Kid do Futebol*'.

He then moved to Cortiba FC, in Paraná state, and was a regular team member in the 1988 Brazilian championship. When Cortiba played Flamengo, Zico was on the opposing team, and approached Kazu at half time. '*Sucesso!*' he said, shaking his hand. 'You've made it!' The Japanese papers in Brazil had a picture the next day of the two together, and called him the pride of Japanese Brazil. Kazu cried when he read the article.

Kazu had indeed made it, and he spent another year in Brazil, playing again for Santos, where he scored the winning goal against Palmeiras in the 1990 Sao Paulo state championship. But Kazu decided he had stayed in Brazil long enough. The impending start of the J.League would enable him to turn professional in his home country. His initial motivation for going to Brazil had been the thrill of watching World Cup videos. If Japanese football improved enough now, he might even get a chance to play in the competition himself.

However, the years in Brazil had changed Kazu, and on his return he immediately caused friction. He started playing for Yomiuri Club in the JSL, and while the other players passed the ball and worked as a team, Kazu tried to dribble with the ball. His teammates didn't like it. One was quoted as saying: 'He's cheeky; he thinks he's the only man on the pitch.' He was no more popular with Yomiuri's coaches, who criticised his lack of team spirit, and played him in just three out of twenty-two JSL games in his first year back. 'He's got technique, but he is not contributing to

47

victory,' said one. 'He has not yet started thinking "for the team".'

Kazu was also full of suggestions for Japanese football as a whole – suggestions that often sounded like complaints. He griped to referees, and about the standard of Japanese refereeing in general. And he was not happy with the running of the national team, which, despite the move to professionalism, was still run along amateur lines – players were still not paid for international appearances. 'In foreign teams they are all paid, and Japan won't be able to win with its current way of doing things,' Kazu explained. 'I knew the environment in Japan and Brazil was different. But if I didn't speak out, Japan would not change.'

Kazu soon began to show his true ability, and Japan's new football fans loved him. His jazzy Rivelino-inspired feints produced screams from female fans. After scoring, he performed a crotch-grabbing, hip-jiggling, arm-waving celebration that was dubbed the 'Kazu dance'. After one goal against Antlers in the 1992 Nabisco Cup, Kazu first hugged all his teammates, then ran to celebrate with the Verdy bench, and finally over to the stands, where he blew kisses to his fans. Zico was playing for Kashima, and was furious both at this performance, and at how the referee appeared to defer to Kazu, running after the star to fetch him back rather than remaining in the centre circle to restart the match. He was so annoyed that he got the Antlers to kick off again without permission from the referee, then fired a shot from forty metres into the Verdy goal. Instead of a goal, the referee awarded him a yellow card.

Kazu was so flamboyant that he was too Brazilian even for a Brazilian. When he was named Most Valuable Player in the 1993 J.League Awards, while all the other recipients turned up in sober black dinner jackets, white shirts and black bow ties, Kazu wore a scarlet suit, white collarless shirt and a black-and-white polka dot scarf. He played his celebrity to perfection, regularly flashing his cocky Tom Cruise grin, and marrying a gorgeous singer-model in a high profile, much-photographed wedding. He also held the J.League's scoring record until 2001, and became the national team's second top scorer ever with fifty-six goals in ninety-one appearances. When the national anthem played before these games, he placed his hand on his heart like an American, and belted out the song with the born-again patriotism of a returnee.

As much as his achievements on the pitch, it was Kazu's story that moved the Japanese – the mediocre talent who went overseas and turned himself into a top athlete through effort and a refusal to give up on a seemingly hopeless cause. He was a returning hero of the kind that legends are made. In his book *The Hero With A Thousand Faces*, mythology scholar Joseph Campbell described the pattern of a hero's journey as found in stories like the *Odyssey*: 'A hero ventures forth from the world of common day into a region of supernatural wonder; fabulous forces are there encountered and a decisive victory is won; the hero comes back from this mysterious adventure with the power to bestow boons on his fellow man.' Kazu had visited, suffered and eventually triumphed in the land of the football gods, and transformed himself into a Japanese with Brazil inside him. He could now bless Japanese football with the powers he had acquired.

CHAPTER THREE

The Football Boom

Publicity for the new league meant plenty of Japanese were curious to go along and find out what the games were like. But that was not the same as creating thousands of loyal supporters who would watch their team every week for years, losing streaks included. And even if they did keep coming, numbers were also no guarantee of the kind of atmosphere generated by fans in the older footballing nations.

These concerns weighed particularly heavily on the Yokohama Flügels. Yokohama, a short train ride from Tokyo through dense commuter suburbs, was the only city to start the J.League with two teams. While the other eight clubs could at least count on hometown support, Yokohama's new fans had a choice between the All Nippon Airways (ANA)-backed Flügels and the Nissan-backed Marinos. Unlike other cities that support more than one football club, Yokohama had none of the obvious divisions that underlie such support. There were no social tensions like those in Buenos Aires that fuel the animosity between River Plate, the team of the privileged, and Boca Juniors, the team of the underprivileged. Nor was the city divided along religious grounds like Glasgow. And neither club would naturally attract supporters from a particular area of the city, as they shared the same ground in the suburbs.

But the sensible option in Yokohama seemed to be the Marinos. As Nissan FC, they had played in Yokohama for years, winning the JSL several times, and had a number of Japan internationals on their books, who were now supplemented by Argentine stars like Diaz. The Flügels had no such history. As ANA FC, they had bounced between divisions one and two of the JSL throughout the 1980s. In search of more support, they even nominated the island of Kyushu, a two-hour flight south-west of Yokohama, as a kind of deputy hometown. They set up a youth team there, and planned to hold nine "home" matches a year in a newly built stadium. In Yokohama, though, no one seemed interested. In the run-up to the J.League's official start, when other teams' cuddly toy mascots and scarves were jumping off CATEGORY-1 shelves, the Flügels' replica kits looked destined for the end-of-season sale.

In the new world of commercially driven football, this was a desperate situation. The Flügels needed fans and their money, and needed them fast. Their salvation arrived in the form of Yoshiharu Yamamoto, a courteous man in his early thirties, though with greying hair that made him look slightly older. As managing director of The First, an event promoter, his main business was setting up ski contests and baseball competitions for students. He also organised side-shows at college football tournaments, inviting former internationals along to take part in kick-around games. At one of these in 1992, he ran into a group of former ANA FC players. They managed to convince themselves and him that he could solve their problems. Here was a man who understood how to win over the nation's youth.

Yamamoto went to see the Flügels play in the 1992 Nabisco Cup, a pre-J.League warm-up event. Like all the new teams, the Flügels attracted a few thousand spectators to each of this series of matches. But their crowd was quieter than elsewhere. When the J.League-proper started in May 1993, Mitsuzawa Stadium, a 15,000-seat open-topped ground, was packed for the Flügels' first home game against Shimizu S-Pulse. But most of the crowd were wearing S-Pulse orange, and carrying Shimizu flags – even though their small town was nearly a hundred miles down the Pacific coast. 'I saw we were being crushed in support,' Yamamoto remembered later. 'We couldn't go on like that.'

So The First started campaigning. It set up ticket stands in Yokohama's shopping malls and Chinatown, an area bordered by two-storey-high Chinese gates and boasting 500 restaurants. The First canvassed for young fans in amusements parks, schools and via the local football association. Yamamoto invited former participants in his college ski trips to come and watch the games. He set up a supporters' club, calling it the Yokohama Jets in keeping with Flügels' aeronautical theme.

With the huge publicity the J.League generated in all Japan's media, the Flügels began to attract healthy crowds. But the atmosphere remained flat. Yamamoto thought the people going to see the Flügels were mainly turning up out of curiosity: all J.League matches were sold out, and the Flügels became known as being relatively easy to get tickets for. Flügels home matches were filled with a greater proportion of women and children than other teams. Some of these blew into what the Japanese called 'cheerphones' – hooters producing a wailing sound that had been popular in continental Europe in the 1970s. Most, however, sat and watched in silence as if they were at the ballet.

Though an extreme case, the Flügels were facing a problem common to all Japan's new football crowds: few people knew what to do. Though the J.League's founders had prepared meticulously for its launch, one crucial element they could not lay on was the atmosphere. American sports like basketball and American football had lots of breaks in play so organisers could blast out Gary Glitter's 'Rock 'n' Roll Pt. 2' to get the crowd shouting along with pompon-shaking cheerleaders, or Queen's 'We Will Rock You' to get them stamping. Football went on for ninety minutes with just one break in the middle, leaving the fans to create the mood for themselves.

Japan had a well-established solution to meet this challenge. Support groups, or *oendan*, first appeared in Japan with the spread of college sports in the late nineteenth century. More than the event, these bands of students were interested in demonstrating loyalty to their school, and they sometimes caused trouble. One of the earliest recorded incidents involved supporters of rival

Tokyo colleges at a boat race in 1890. One group waved white flags, while the other waved red flags. At some point, a ruckus broke out and the race was cancelled for the next few years. Years later, *oendan* attached themselves to each of Japan's twelve professional baseball teams. As well as leading crowd chants with drums and trumpets, some of these let off balloons as an extra push at the start of the seventh innings. One innovative group even opened plastic umbrellas before the seventh, and to celebrate home-runs.

In high schools, *oendan* became a highly regarded extra-curricular activity. Instead of playing football or baseball, students could enter the *oendan* and practise supporting their school team for inter-school baseball or football tournaments. Both college and high school *oendan* were ordered by rank and seniority, and marked by militaristic tendencies. They learned arm movements a bit like tribal war dances, grunting as they threw synchronised punches in the air. The core male group was surrounded by mini-skirted girls waving pompons. Most *oendan* had brass bands that played upbeat tunes, ranging from old military songs to 'Popeye The Sailor Man'. Even at the end of the twentieth century, the boys often wore traditional Japanese school uniforms to games – black trousers and tunics modelled on nineteenth-century Prussian army uniforms. To this they might add a kamikaze-style white headband with a red sun and the word '*hisshou*' – 'victory at all costs'.

While the new football fans could borrow the essential *oendan* organisation, they did not want to sound like the established baseball crowds. Baseball crowds were well-organised, with drummers and trumpeters who led chants of 'Knock it out [hitter's name]!' whenever their team was at bat. But one of the J.League's early attractions was its contrast with existing Japanese sports events. Many football fans considered baseball old-fashioned and middle-aged, and wanted to put some distance between the two games. So the more active fans did what the Japanese have often done when they want to learn something new. They looked around the world to see who did it best.

Japanese football had played at adopt-a-country before. Since the 1960s West Germany had been the model. First, a German coach, Cramer, trained the national team for the 1964 and 1968 Olympics. Yasuhiko Okudera played in the Bundesliga from the late 1970s, other top players like Kunishige Kamamoto went there to train, and coaches like Takeshi Okada, the 1998 World Cup team manager, studied there. In the 1980s Brazil started to take over as an influence, as teenagers went there to become club trainees, and Brazilians arrived to play in the JSL. When it came to learning how to be football fans, there were two main styles to choose from: the pulsating samba crowds of Brazil, and the chants and songs of Europe and Argentina. For some clubs the decision was obvious. Verdy Kawasaki had a mock-Brazilian name, and had several players who were either Brazilian or had lived there – they went for samba. Others, like Urawa Reds and the Marinos, who had many German and Argentine players, were more attracted by the singing and chanting approach.

Yokohama Flügels were not clear where they were getting their football from. The manager was Japanese, and the first head coach a Slovenian. But they got their tactics from Italy, playing a 4-4-2 'zone press' – shrinking the distance between their forwards and the defensive line to maintain superior numbers in midfield. Coaches showed the players videos of AC Milan, the experts at this technique and Europe's top team at the time. None of the imported players were Italian, though; they were Brazilians and Argentines. The Japanese goalkeeper had permed his hair into dreadlocks. Even the team name – AS Flügels – was a confusing multinational hotchpotch. Though Flügel was a German word, an 's' was added to make an English-style plural. The 'AS' came from the owners' names, ANA and construction company Sato Kogyo, combined to sound like the beginning of Italian club AS Roma.

So while Yamamoto knew he wanted to form a support group, he was not sure what kind of noise it should make. By the time the J.League started, he had gathered a group of about thirty fans, and they began to support with drums, chants and hand-claps. But the other spectators, often families with young children, were too shy to shout along, and the support didn't spread. He looked at the different styles being tried around the country, and asked other supporters' groups for tips on leading a crowd. He learnt the best positions for crowd orchestration: flag-bearers stood at the front so they had room to wave their banners for goal celebrations, and ripple them in anger at a bad call by the referee; the leader stood like a conductor in the middle of the stands, sometimes with deputies spread out to the sides. The fans of several teams were playing samba in the stands, and Yamamoto saw samba could whip up a good noise without people having to raise their voices. Around the fifth match, Yamamoto bought four samba drums for the Jets. The top Jets members beat out a samba rhythm, and before long even mothers with toddlers started clapping along.

The Jets soon gathered a following drawn to the Flügels for a variety of reasons. Some were tactics connoisseurs who liked the zone press. Some were fans of THE ALFEE, a Flügels-supporting rock trio that had been turning out hit albums since the late seventies. Others said they liked the aeroplane theme. Lots of women came to watch skilful young midfielder Masakiyo Maezono, whose sulky, unshaven good looks made him obvious heartthrob material. One fan even gave the reason as dislike of Yokohama Marinos' owner Nissan, because a Nissan car salesman had once been rude to his father. From about thirty members at the opening of the J.League, the Jets grew to 1,000 by the end of 1993. By the following year they numbered 2,500.

True, the Jets music wasn't Sergio Mendez – or even anything Brazilians would recognise as samba. Yamamoto admitted 'we were just amateurs'. But for the time being it worked. Later, when Yamamoto wanted to crank up the rhythms coming from the stand, he would ask advice from the professional samba musician who led the support at nearby Verdy Kawasaki.

Verdy were the early kings of the J.League. They had been a cut above the rest since the days of the JSL, when they played as the first team of Yomiuri Football Club. Though owned by Japan's biggest newspaper, Yomiuri Club operated like a sports club, which children could join to receive coaching. While most other JSL teams had played long-ball football in the German style, Yomiuri was dominated by a pair of talented Brazilians. The club had even paid a samba band to provide support.

For the J.League era, Yomiuri was determined to establish for itself the same dominance of football as it already had in baseball, where its Tokyo Giants were overwhelmingly the most popular team in the land. Verdy signed the core of Japan's national team and paid them handsomely. Both Kazu Miura and Ruy Ramos, a Brazilian who had taken Japanese nationality, earned at least 100 million yen (£600,000) a year, even more than the Giants' top baseball player. Verdy's total annual salary bill came to 1.4 billion yen (£9 million). 'Professional football won't survive without stars, and stars have to be made,' said Yomiuri president Tsuneo Watanabe. 'To generate interest you have to invest up-front, and if you think of it as money spent on publicity, 100 million yen is not that much.' In a speech to Verdy staff just before the J.League started, the president of Yomiuri's broadcasting arm Nippon Television declared that success for Japanese football required one strong club that all the others wanted to beat – just as the Giants had pulled along Japanese baseball. That club was, of course, Verdy.

Though Verdy adopted Kawasaki as its hometown, this was just because the only adequate football ground in Tokyo was the National Stadium, which no one team could be allowed to monopolise. Kawasaki was an industrial town wedged between the capital and Yokohama, and made a convenient alternative. But Kawasaki was also very unfashionable, and Verdy held as many home matches as possible in the National Stadium. Its real ambition could be seen in the badge on the team shirts: 'Verdy – Yomiuri – FC Nippon'. Verdy wanted to represent the whole country.

Verdy's support was on a different level from the rest of the league. A few months into the first season, the club asked Mario Yamaguchi, a Latin soul musician in his late forties, to form a new samba group. Yamaguchi was a professional recording artist who had worked for several years in New York, and the sounds he produced in the stands were the jazziest in the J.League. He called his group *'Camisa Doze'* – 'Twelfth Shirt' – after the Sao Paulo Corinthians' supporters group which thought its support was equivalent to having a twelfth player on the field. Yamaguchi ordered over 2,000 samba tambourines and 100 drums from Brazil, custom-made with 'Camisa Doze' printed on them. As well as playing along at matches, Camisa Doze released three CD singles and an album of Verdy samba, making the mistake of asking a player, Ruy Ramos, to write awful Portuguese lyrics:

> Superstars – Amigos, Amigas, Amigos!
> Verdy – take us up in a whirlwind of excitement,
> Like a hurricane!

Even this was not quite as bad as the attempt by Pele, whom they commissioned earlier to write lyrics for a team song. The old master, displaying considerably less talent than he had with a football, came up with:

> Ole, Ole, Ole Ola.
> Hey, Verdy, fantastic technique!
> Come everyone, and have a good time together,
> Together with Verdy – kick-off time!

Besides the samba, the other distinctive noise from the Verdy crowd was screaming. Unlike football teams almost anywhere else in the world, Verdy attracted more women than men, and about 10,000 of Camisa Doze's 16,000 peak membership were female. Many of them were schoolgirls who thought football was new and exotic – the latest craze after Louis Vuitton bags – and they treated matches like pop concerts. They tapped away at tambourines, and erupted in squeals when the ball came to the handsome Kazu. Football became so popular with women that sports shops sometimes displayed replica shirts on mannequins with breasts. Many of the outnumbered men appeared to go to matches to pick up girls rather than watch the football: Yamaguchi knew of at least three married couples who met watching Verdy.

The Verdy atmosphere was polite in the extreme. Fans cleared rubbish from the stands after each match, and never booed opposing teams. In fact, they applauded opposing players when they did well. 'After all,' reasoned Yamaguchi, 'that player might come to Verdy one day.' They chanted the opposing team's name before kick-off to show friendly intentions, and the rival supporters usually chanted back. When Verdy played away to other teams with courteous fans, like Hiroshima Sanfrecce and S-Pulse, those support-ers would get to the stadium early and save a block of unreserved seats for the samba band. Yamaguchi encour-aged children and the disabled to come and join in. He was particularly pleased when a deaf child came along with his mother and played a drum by feeling the beat through his stomach. Playing music for the first time, Yamaguchi remembered, the boy's face lit up with happiness, bringing tears of joy to his mother's eyes.

Even if Verdy was an extreme case, most Japanese football matches were pleasant affairs. They ended with the two sides lining up side by side in the middle of the pitch and waving towards the main stand. Then the players went over to greet the supporters, standing in a row on the goal-line and bowing in unison. There followed a 'hero interview' with the man of the match, his thoughts on the game broadcast over the public address system. Japan appeared to have created a nicer version of football, keeping all the fun parts but leaving out the ugliness – the bad manners and hooliganism – that dogged it elsewhere.

Just as the J.League was taking off, Japan discovered even more football excitement in the exploits of the national team. Two years before the start of the league, chairman Kawabuchi was head of the JFA's development committee and was wondering who to appoint as the next national team coach. He had coached the national team himself for four months in 1980 and 1981, and thought there was one big problem with the position: like the players in those days, Japanese coaches were corporate amateurs who did not make all their living from football. National team coaches were, moreover, on sabbatical from the companies that paid their salaries. However much effort they made, however much they sacrificed time with their families and progress up the corporate ladder, when they failed to qualify for the World Cup or to win even an Asian tournament, they shrugged their shoulders and went back to their comfortable jobs at the office.

That had been accepted in the past; when most of the Japanese public had been uninterested in football, no one expected any more. But the advent of professionalism would create new public expectations for the national team, and one of the league's founding aims was to raise Japanese football to the level where Japan qualified regularly for the World Cup. Indeed, with the first round of the 1994 World Cup qualifiers starting in April 1993, the month before the J.League's grand opening, Kawabuchi was also hoping that a successful campaign would give the league a valuable boost.

With all this in mind, Kawabuchi turned his thoughts back to Dettmar Cramer, and the only time Japanese football had achieved any degree of success. He reached the conclusion that until the professional era was properly established, a Japanese coach in charge of the national team would not be as effective as a foreigner. Looking around the world, he first considered big-name coaches, and informally sounded out Carlos Bilardo, who had led Argentina to victory in the 1986 World Cup, and Tele Santana, coach of the creative but unsuccessful Brazil sides of 1982 and 1986. But he abandoned the idea when they said they wanted to bring their own staff at great expense. What's more,

Kawabuchi thought Japanese football was not ready for the sophistication of such world-class coaches. On a scale of one to ten, with top-level world football at ten, Kawabuchi gave Japan about five. More than a Bilardo or a Santana, the Japan team would benefit from a coach that taught the basics as Cramer had.

Before he became involved in football full-time, Kawabuchi had worked for Furukawa Electric Co. as head of its metal sales department. Posted in Nagoya, on weekends he appeared as a football analyst on a local TV station in nearby Shizuoka prefecture, the one place in Japan where the game was already popular. In 1982, he noticed a big improvement in the football team run by motorbike maker Yamaha. Recently relegated to the JSL's second division, Yamaha not only came top of this, but also knocked out first division sides to win the Emperor's Cup. Enquiring the reason for the improvement, Kawabuchi was told it was thanks to a Dutch coach called Hans Ooft.

Ooft had played professionally as a striker for a number of clubs including Feyenoord, but his career was cut short by injury at the age of twenty-nine. He became a coach, and worked for the Dutch football association, mainly with youth teams. When Yamaha asked him to help them out for a while, he only had time to coach them for two months in the summer of 1982. But even this short period had fundamentally changed the way the team played. A year later, Mazda's football team was relegated to division two, and they too called on Ooft to help them out. He coached Mazda for two years, helping them to gain promotion.

In 1988, Ooft became part of the general management of FC Utrecht, and in September 1991, when Kawabuchi took the new J.League general managers on their study tour of Europe, Ooft made a presentation. Based on this and his observations nearly a decade earlier, Kawabuchi asked Ooft to coach Japan's national team. In May 1992, his appointment was announced, and Ooft addressed a press conference: 'The reason I have come here again is to make sure Japan qualify for the 1994 World Cup in the USA.'

The biggest problem Ooft identified was a cultural one. He felt the players were too quiet during games. They didn't talk to one another. Clearly Japanese hierarchy and discipline did not produce good teamwork in football. 'If you are behind me, then I need you to tell me what to do because you can see better,' he explained. 'But in Japanese culture, you can't do this if the person you are shouting at is older than you. I admire Japanese culture. But you need soccer culture on the pitch.'

The solution was a simple tactical vision that became known as 'Ooft's compact soccer'. He drew a map of the field showing how to bring the defensive line forward to create an offside trap and reduce the area of active play to a length of field between thirty and forty metres. With all the players in this area, the team could pressure the opposition harder. Another map split the field into three areas: the area up front where you can take lots of risks, that in the middle where you can take a few, and that at the back where safety takes priority. Most important of all, he split the field into different areas of responsibility for each team position. These maps meant that all the players had the same picture in their mind of what the team should be doing. 'If they have the same picture in mind, they can start coaching each other,' said Ooft. 'They can say, "Hey, what are you doing!" no matter how old they are.'

Next Ooft taught the Japan team to play in threes. Instead of just a passer and receiver, a pass should also involve a third player who pulled the opposition aside and created space. He told them to look at each other's faces for cues to movement. It formed a holy trinity of ideas they had to remember at all times: Triangle, Eye Contact and Coaching.

Ooft was the next in a long line of foreign teachers bringing western ideas to Japan, and writer Takeo Goto neatly summed up his role: 'The foreign experts who first came to Japan were not, for example, top architects, but rather engineers who were close to the construction site. After this ground work had been completed, real architects came to Japan, and Meiji architectural culture bloomed.' Ooft, said Goto, was the first kind of expert – teaching Japan the basics. 'Using simple English words like " . . . eye contact and triangle", Ooft explained basic tactics to players, coaches and football journalists, and got them to understand it. As a result of these efforts, now [four years afterwards] even regular fans understand the movements of a defensive midfielder.'

The company players Ooft had coached during his first stays in Japan had been impressed by this Dutch football science. But the national team players were more impatient. With football's popularity on the rise with the eager anticipation of the J.League, they had recently gained a new status. The game had acquired an image of individual skills and artistry, and crowds and TV highlights programmes were clear about what they did and did not like to see on the pitch: intelligent positioning and efficient pass work were dull; fancy play was fun. Ooft, however, made the players go through endless repetitions of basic techniques.

The players grew restive, whispering among themselves that Ooft's methods were 'like junior school training', and that he might have spent too long in Holland as a youth coach. Under Ooft, practice games were punctuated by blasts of a whistle, as he stopped the game to give the players more detailed instructions. They muttered under their breath, '*Urusei na – wakatteru yo!*' – 'Yes, yes, I know!' Or they smiled at Ooft politely, while saying in Japanese, 'Oh no, what does he want now!'

Ooft's response to this griping was to drum his message into them more thoroughly. He held lots of meetings, and explained team roles to each player individually. According to Eijun Kiyokumo, the coach working under Ooft, 'The Japanese cannot thoroughly exchange opinions on things, and often just say to each other "*wakatta na?*" – "OK?" – followed by "*wakarimashita*" – "got it". But then they make the same mistake again in a game.' So Ooft made sure they did what he said. When a player replied, '*wakatta*' –

'understood' – he asked them to repeat what he had said to check they had really understood. Then he explained once or twice more until he was sure the message had got through. 'They say "*hai*" – "yes" – and that should mean they understand you,' said Ooft. 'But whether or not they follow what you've said is another matter.'

The first test for Ooft's Japan team came in August 1992 in Beijing, venue for the Dynasty Cup tournament between Japan, South Korea, North Korea and China. Japanese football had for decades been poor even by Asian standards, and South Korea had been a special barrier – the team that always seemed to stop Japan qualifying for the World Cup. In spite of regular friendly matches, Japan had not beaten them for seven years.

Before kick-offs, Ooft usually summarised the opposition's strengths and weaknesses to let the team know what to expect. But this time, when he was given the Korean team sheet, he simply read out the players' names – and then ripped the paper up. He tore it into little pieces, threw them on the floor, and trampled on them, all with a calm expression on his face. 'They have to play us,' he declared. The players were stunned, and Captain Tetsuji Hashiratani told the others: 'Let's forget about past South Korea matches.'

The Koreans were physically stronger, but Japan's new teamwork enabled them to soak up the pressure to earn a 0–0 draw, the first time in twenty-two meetings they had stopped South Korea from scoring. Japan went on to the Dynasty Cup final, where they drew with South Korea a second time. Winning the penalty shoot-out gave Japan their first ever victory in an official international tournament since the Asian Football Confederation was formed in 1954.

After this Japan never looked back. A few months later they won the Asia Cup for the first time. In 1993, they cruised through the first round of World Cup qualifiers, then headed to Doha in Qatar for the final round, where six countries would compete for the two World Cup places available to Asia.

Japan started badly, drawing 0–0 with Saudi Arabia, and losing 2–1 to Iran. But they then beat North Korea 3–0, and, best of all, their old rivals the South by 1–0. With one game remaining in the group, Japan were top with five points, ahead of Saudi Arabia on goal difference. South Korea, Iraq and Iran all had four points. Victory for Japan over Iraq in their last game would take them to America – as would a draw in the unlikely event that South Korea failed to beat the North.

Since the beginning of the J.League the whole of Japan had begun to root for the national team. For the Dynasty Cup in Beijing just a handful of reporters had turned up to Ooft's press conferences. At the Asia Cup the number had risen to several dozen. By the final World Cup qualifiers there were over a hundred. Nearly sixty per cent of the population tuned in to watch on TV, and around one thousand had travelled to Doha, and they waved flags and set up a banner saying, 'Win To Go USA 94'.

Trained by Ooft and egged on by this support, Japan were flying. After just six minutes, they hit the bar, and Kazu headed in the rebound. They kept this lead for the rest of the half, and went into the break 1–0 ahead. At halftime, the players were so worked up that Ooft found it hard to get through to them. In the end he only managed one message, which he wrote with a magic marker on a large sheet of paper: '45 MINS TO USA'. Ten minutes into the second half, Iraq equalised, and then went on the attack. But Japan defended hard, and with twenty-one minutes to go staged a counterattack. Masashi Nakayama scored. All they had to now do was hold on.

Dettmar Cramer had been impressed with the 1968 team's ultimate display of the Japanese spirit, but he thought they still lacked one kind of samurai discipline. They did not have the instinct to kill off an opponent. One quality Cramer had read about in his samurai studies was *zanshin* – a word constructed out of kanji characters meaning 'remain' and 'heart'. One day, he told his Japan team that they lacked this *zanshin*. None of them had heard the word (it is not featured even in quite large modern Japanese dictionaries), and they looked at each other in puzzlement. So he explained: '*Zanshin* is in the Japanese way of the sword, isn't it? It looks good if you take a sweeping cut at someone, and then just turn your back. But the fallen victim might summon up his last morsel of strength, and come back at you. So after you've taken a sweeping cut, you must remain alert until he has taken his last breath. That is *zanshin*. Japanese soccer does not have that.'

In the dying minutes of the game in Doha, Iraq had lost all chance of qualifying for the World Cup, but for some reason they were still fighting like demons. The Japanese players had heard a rumour that Saddam Hussein had threatened that if they lost to Japan, they would be whipped or forced to join the army and serve on the front line as punishment. Still the Japanese players couldn't believe it. Defender Masami Ihara even started shouting at the Iraqis in a mixture of Japanese and broken English whenever he was competing for a ball or there was a break in play: 'We go to the World Cup,' he told them. 'You can't.' Ruy Ramos was a creative midfielder, who rarely defended and never did anything as vulgar and un-Brazilian as simply clear the ball. But even he sprinted back into his own half at one point to pick up a loose ball and boot it into touch. In fact that was pretty much all the Japanese were doing: struggling to get the ball off the Iraqis, then hoofing it away upfield, for a throw or for a corner. There had been few stoppages in the game, and when ninety minutes were up, the travelling fans were as excited as the players. They began chanting faster than before as they prepared to celebrate the greatest triumph in the nation's football history.

But instead, what followed was the most terrible moment in Japanese football – a reversal that became known in later years as 'The Doha Tragedy'. A few seconds into injury time, Iraq got a corner. They took it short, an Iraqi dribbled round Kazu, and crossed the ball high to the edge of the goal area. Omran jumped above the Japanese defence and met the ball with his head. He flicked it at a perfect angle, so it flew out of reach of goalkeeper Shigetatsu Matsunaga, across the goal, and into the far side of the net.

Some Japanese players simply collapsed on the pitch, and couldn't pick themselves up again even as Ramos ran forward with the ball to the centre spot. After the restart, he quickly passed the ball out to the right. It went out of play. Then the referee blew the final whistle, and the Japanese team fell to the ground. South Korea had beaten the North, and Japan were out of the World Cup. For a few minutes the players sat numbly on the turf, or stood up to walk around in a daze, unable to comprehend what had happened. Then it registered, and one by one they started crying.

Painful as this defeat was for the nation, it was also magnificent drama. Years later some fans even wore commemorative T-shirts showing a clock registering the exact time at which Iraq scored the fateful equaliser. Though qualification would have been better, the match showed the Japanese the range of emotions football could incite, and made the game even more popular than before. Besides, to have got as far as Japan did was an achievement in itself.

The bright start to professional football in Japan resonated with a brief mood of national renewal. After three decades of expansion had made the economy the main source of national pride, in 1992 growth hit a wall: the Nikkei stock market average had already fallen to less than half its 1989 bubble economy peak, and then GDP began to contract. Then in the summer of 1993, Japan looked like it was turning a corner. The electorate booted out the conservative Liberal Democratic Party after four decades of corrupt, secretive administration when it had been tolerated largely because it seemed irrelevant – bureaucrats ran the country so well that it didn't seem to matter which politicians were nominally in power. The LDP was replaced by a coalition masterminded by Ichiro Ozawa, a politician whose rallying cry was to make Japan a 'normal' nation, free of all the cronyism and stifling regulations that hampered its progress. The new prime minister, Morihiro Hosokawa, was dapper, made speeches in English, and at fifty-five was relatively young. That same summer, the emperor's son, Crown Prince Naruhito, married a pretty, intelligent woman. An ancient religious ceremony in traditional dress was followed by an open-topped drive through Tokyo in western wedding clothes. Four years after the death of the wartime emperor, Hirohito, the stuffy imperial dynasty appeared to be striking a nice balance between tradition and a more cheerful modernity. The whole nation seemed ready to transform itself and thrive to a merrier tune. Fresh, young and international, the J.League was like a harbinger of a new era.

From early concerns about how to promote the J.League, football became almost too popular. Jumping on a wave of enthusiasm, guests on TV variety shows peppered their banter with football vocabulary: unfair gibes at others were 'offside', and sometimes merited a 'yellow card' from the emcee. Until a year earlier the tabloid sports newspapers had been dominated by baseball, followed by sumo and horse racing. While whole pages were sometimes devoted to angling, football was usually shoved into corners next to other minor sports like volleyball and rugby. With the J.League however, football grabbed more front pages than baseball. The insides of the papers detailed every match using diagrams with straight, squiggly and dotted lines to show the dribbles, off-the-ball runs and through-passes that led to goals. A person's sporting preference began to form part of his or her identity, making some baseball fans feel threatened by the new cultural invasion. When TV shows asked guests whether they were part of the baseball-faction or the football-faction, the baseballers said things like 'football doesn't have enough goals'. The football people said, 'baseball is dull because it isn't as fast as football'. Defending his sport after a 'sayonara, come-from-behind victory home run', one baseball announcer yelled with satisfaction: 'See how interesting baseball is! You don't get this kind of scene in football!'

A spin-off industry for J.League merchandise exploded as Sony Creative developed 1,700 branded products in the league's first year. Over one million flags were sold, with more serious fans buying special vinyl quivers to carry them. Caps, cuddly team characters, and team scarves (made out of towelling rather than wool because of Japan's sweaty summer weather) were snapped up as soon as they reached the shops, as were Brazilian-style woven bracelets worn to bring luck. Plastic megaphones were made in two sections, with a joint in the middle near the mouth-end: when you slapped them they made a loud clacking sound. Cheerphones were so popular they provoked complaints from residents near stadiums, and manufacture was halted in the summer. Mizuno opened 700 outlets called J.STA-TION to sell replica shirts, and shifted 200,000 in the first four months. The league's first-stage sponsor Suntory put team logos on cans of Malts brand beer for sale in J.League hometowns, and sold plain 'J.League Malts' everywhere else. In the six months to July, 1993, it shifted more than double the quantity of beer of the previous year, despite an unusually cool summer that dented the overall market. Then there were J.League crisps to eat with your beer. There was J.League chewing gum, J.League chocolate, J.League ready-made curry, cup noodles and cornflakes. Electrical companies produced J.League batteries and J.League character watches. All were a runaway success, and to buy them you could get your money out of the bank with a Fuji Bank J.League cash card, or pay later by Nicos J.League credit card. The 'J' in the name was so popular that over the next years it would be taken up by other unrelated products, where its 'new Japan' connotations produced a fresh, international image. Domestic music was labelled 'J-pop' in record stores. A brand of mobile phone called itself 'J-Phone'. And domestic beef producers defended market share against American and Australian imports by labelling their product 'J beef'. At the end of 1993, *Nikkei Trendy*, a magazine covering advertising and marketing trends, named the J.League its Brand of the Year. Business author Awata thought the image was so strong that 'the J.League is a character, just like Mickey Mouse and Snoopy.'

The effect was a kind of economic alchemy. Instead of just selling tickets to pay club wages and expenses, the new sports marketing techniques multiplied the money like magic. Selling TV rights not only made money for the league, but publicised it and raised the value of advertising boards round the pitch. The J.League product makers paid a licence fee while filling convenience stores with the J.League logo. Star players went on TV and in magazines, promoting pep drinks (Kazu), consumer finance (Lineker) and toupees (the balding Brazilian Alcindo). All kept the public focused on football. According to another economic writer, Yukio Ubukata, more than a sports event 'the J.League [was] a kind of media ... like TV and radio.' Estimates for the size of the J.League market – the money put into everything from new facilities to sponsorship deals – started at 110 billion yen (about £700 million), with Ubukata coming up with 210.7 billion (about £1.3 billion). Less than a tenth of this total came from gate receipts, and over a third from licensed products.

J.League fever swept the land, and because most stadiums held only the required minimum of 15,000 spectators, tickets were scarce. People queued up outside ticket agencies from before dawn, but even this was no guarantee of success, and many went home disappointed after hours of waiting. This too became news, making even more people want to see the matches. In Grampus hometown Nagoya, there was even a report that someone had been murdered over a J.League ticket, when the victim's body was found floating in that city's harbour. For those who couldn't get tickets, the TV networks showed games in primetime, getting ratings that averaged more than 15 per cent throughout the first year. 'It's a great success,' was how chairman Kawabuchi summed up the league's start. 'Over 100 points,' he gave it in some imaginary ratings system. 'To be honest it feels more like 200 points.'

It really was that good. And asked their favourite sport, an increasing number of Japanese replied 'J.League'. But was this the same as football?

CHAPTER FOUR

The Way Of The Football Supporter

The Japanese tend to believe there is a correct way to do everything. They go to classes to learn how to arrange flowers, and read manuals explaining the right way to answer a telephone (bow as you would when greeting someone normally, and raise the pitch of your voice). In earlier times soldiering developed into the Way of the Samurai, while making tea became a ceremony. Modern Japanese companies instruct their recruits in bowing – ranging from fifteen degrees for an immediate boss up to forty-five for a major client – and where four people of different status should sit in a car. So when professional football first came to Japan, most of the people involved were determined to do it the correct way. As well as supporters and the J.League organisation itself, that also applied to a few managers running J.League clubs who were determined to form the right kind of relationship between club and supporters.

The man who got it most right was Hitoshi Sato, a manager at Urawa Reds. A thirty-minute train ride from central Tokyo, Urawa was known as a 'dormitory town', because living there usually meant no more than sleeping after work and playing in the capital. Asked where they came from by people from other parts of Japan, Urawa residents just said 'Tokyo' to avoid having to explain. Sato had a clear vision of how you turned this kind of place into a town of football supporters: by generating a bit of local pride where there was none.

Sato was an exception. Despite Japanese football's new image and scale, J.League clubs were mostly run by their owners' sales or marketing staff rather than specialised sports administrators. After a few years running the football team, these managers would return to their original careers at a car or electronics company. While they were interested in football, few had any idea of the reasons fans go back to watch their local team week after week. But Sato knew exactly why. He first got hooked on football as a child. Every Saturday night he watched *Diamond Soccer*, a TV programme that showed part of a European football match, usually English or West German. More than the game itself, he loved the atmosphere – the packed crowds surging forward on the terraces, and the songs echoing under stadium roofs. When he was sixteen he decided to see it himself, and started working part-time to save the necessary money. By his third year of university, in 1978, he had saved one million yen (then about £3,000), and he took off for London and a trip round Europe. 'Those three months were like a dream,' he remembered later. 'I had never watched football standing up before. It was a full house, and the supporters were singing, waving flags and holding up scarves. It was everything I had seen on TV but I was actually there.'

First he went to Nottingham to see Forest play Liverpool. Small, very skinny and barely able to speak English, he stopped a couple of boys his own age to ask directions to the City Ground. They were going to the match too, so they bought him a meat pie and took him along. At Maine Road, Manchester, he handed a notebook and pen to Manchester City supporters and they wrote down for him the words to the song they were singing. Across town, a kindly United official spotted him taking photographs of Old Trafford from the street. The official invited him in to see the boot, medical and dressing rooms, then took him out onto the pitch, and let him sit on the team bench. Sato then took off for the Continent, visiting West Germany and Spain. He returned to Japan with photos of himself posing with two of the great players of that era – Kevin Keegan, then of Hamburg SV, and Johann Cruyff of Barcelona – as well as a record of Liverpool players singing 'You'll Never Walk Alone', 'Liverpool Lou', 'We Shall Not

Be Moved' and 'We Can Do It'. More importantly though, he brought back an instinct for what made football work: the pride and generosity of the people who had showed him round came from a feeling that the club was somehow theirs. Whoever formally owned the teams and grounds, in a deeper sense the clubs belonged to the towns-people.

Sato's interest in football led to a dream career break. Having joined Mitsubishi Motors Corporation out of college, he qualified as a referee (third class) and officiated at company matches. When his eyesight weakened he supported the company team instead: Mitsubishi Football Club. At some away matches he and a colleague were the only supporters to turn up. They picked up stray balls during the pre-match warm-up, then sat in the stands and waved flags. Eventually this dogged loyalty paid off in an unexpected way. When Mitsubishi Motors decided to enter the J.League with a team based in Urawa, they asked Sato to become general secretary.

Sato decided to design a real football club from scratch. Normally called Urawa Red Diamonds, or just Urawa Reds, the club's full name was Mitsubishi Urawa Football Club – MUFC, just like Manchester United Football Club. Remembering his trip to the Manchester United ground, Sato decided to give Urawa Reds the same colours: red shirts, white shorts and black socks. He had 'Play to the limit' written on the shirts, a favourite phrase of the legendary United manager Sir Matt Busby. With the help of a British teacher living in Urawa, he penned a club song in English to the tune of Rod Stewart's 'Sailing':

> We are Diamonds, we are Diamonds,
> Yes we love you, boys in red.
> We stand beside you, forever always,
> Yes red Diamonds, you're the best.
>
> We are Diamonds, we are Diamonds,
> All together, hand in hand.

We will keep on, singing for you,
Yes red Diamonds, you're the best.

Sato was tireless in his devotion. He studied European supporters clubs, looking at the yearbooks produced by Bayern Munich and Juventus. In these, he noticed branches listed all over Europe. Thinking the Japanese would be too shy to apply to such groups, he decided to let three or more people set up and register an Official Supporters Club. They would pay 800 yen (£5), enough to cover the cost of a nylon Reds flag and the package and posting. He produced an annual club handbook, which listed the supporters clubs and featured smiling player portraits, a match-day programme for each home game (something else he had noticed in Europe), and he encouraged fans to send in letters so they could influence club affairs. When the Reds lost too many matches in their early days, he stood with a megaphone in front of a stand of angry supporters and addressed their complaints.

Sato dealt with crowd trouble in ways designed not to alienate fans. At a match against Nagoya Grampus, some Reds supporters ran onto the pitch to protest a goal disallowed for offside, and a middle-aged drunk threw something at the Nagoya manager. Sato could have imposed new rules or roped off the front part of the stands, as Tokyo's National Stadium had done following a similar incident several years earlier. But he opposed measures that might create a rift between club and supporters, and instead produced a leaflet. It featured a picture of a player with his arm round a young fan, with the words: 'You and me – let's create great football together!' Below this was a message of thanks for the fine atmosphere produced by the Reds supporters – along with some rules: no fireworks, no smoke bombs, no invading the pitch. 'Please sing along with the Reds supporters song,' the leaflet finished. 'This will be broadcast at halftime. Lyrics are printed on the back.'

Perhaps most important was his reaction to the fantastic early success of the J.League, when every match was sold out and people queued for tickets in central Urawa from before dawn. Sato decided to discriminate in favour of Urawa residents, setting up a phone reservation system that could only be dialled from local numbers. 'All the time I thought about how to create an atmosphere like I had seen in Europe,' he explained. 'I didn't want anyone to be disappointed in football.'

Urawa had been keen on football for longer than most of the rest of Japan. The area surrounding Urawa had a long history of schools' football, and the town had won a J.League franchise only after waging a long campaign that eventually led to an introduction to Mitsubishi Motors. From a series of pre-J.League warm-up games, local youths assembled on the terrace at the home supporters' end of the town's Komaba Stadium. They held mini-conferences, putting together ideas from overseas football they had seen on TV, and talking about how to make their stadium fizz.

They named themselves Crazy Calls, and quickly developed an unmatched repertoire of original chants, songs and visual displays. About ten minutes before kick-off, they started to sing themselves into the right mood for the team's current form. The Reds would come bottom in both stages of the 1993 season and the first stage of 1994, and during losing streaks they hummed Elvis's 'I Can't Help Falling In Love With You' – a hit for UB40 at the time – to express their undying devotion. Coming off rare victories they hummed 'Land Of Hope And Glory' to salute their glorious progress. Minutes before the start they sent a war-cry round the stadium – a chorus inspired by chants they had heard at rock concerts, and which they called 'Warrior'. It began the same as the chant in Slade's 1981 single 'We'll Bring The House Down': one supporter shouted 'Ooh–ooh–ooh Ooh–ooh!' through a megaphone, and thousands of voices replied in unison. They decked the stadium with banners saying things like 'Red or Dead'. In a later innovation, fans draped a huge banner, featuring a red heart on a white background, from the second tier of the side stand so it nearly reached the ground. Then, in a kabuki-style flourish, they dropped this away to reveal its reverse, a white heart on a red background. Inside the hearts was written the number 12: 'We are the twelfth player, who will help you to victory,' it told their team. When the referee blew for kick-off, streamers and confetti made from ripped up newspapers exploded from the stands to a burst of: 'Ur-a-wa, Come on, come on, come on! / Ur-a-wa, Come on, come on, come on! / Ur-a-wa ...'

The Reds' supporters' ardour went beyond the shows they put on. In contrast to the nice manners at Verdy, they set out to be the hard men of the J.League. Late in 1993 Crazy Calls banned women from the key support area behind the goal. Shouts of encouragement to players in 'yellow voices' had little effect as support, they reasoned; it was young men's deeper, rougher, louder voices that damaged the opposition's spirit. 'We didn't really mind having girls around,' explained Koichi Yoshizawa, their first leader, 'but our image was getting soft.' The standard of refereeing was poor in the league's first year, and after one match several angry supporters burst into the referee's changing room, only to find he had already run away. Japan's sports tabloids revelled in this kind of incident, and after this and a series of pitch invasions they quickly pinned the label 'hooligan' on the Reds' followers.

Crazy Calls' biggest departure was booing their own players. Booing not only violated Japanese society's funda-mental rule of politeness, it also contradicted basic assump-tions about sport that had grown up in schools and companies: players were always believed to be trying their best; and losing didn't much matter anyway. Said Don Goodman, a onetime West Bromwich Albion striker who played for Hiroshima Sanfrecce before returning to Britain to play for clubs including Walsall: 'After being beaten comfortably at home once, the Hiroshima crowd still applauded and cheered. This was very strange because in England you can get booed off by your own supporters.' And if a striker missed an easy chance, adoring girl fans would chant his name to comfort and revive him instead of whistling disapproval or inquiring loudly what he was being paid for. When teams came over to bow in front of the stands after a match, fans usually sang and waved flags in encouragement and thanks even if they had lost. When one (male) Verdy fan booed Kazu Miura for missing a penalty, the girls nearby leapt to his defence and began a 'Ka-zu! Ka-zu!' chant to make up for the rudeness. Kazu himself, who had learnt his football overseas, thought this treatment a little strange. 'Playing football in Brazil, the spectators' booing was really frightening,' he said. 'But in the J.League you get applauded even when you make a mistake. I always think, is this really good enough?' The Reds supporters thought not, and held their players up to professional standards. Losing to Gamba Osaka in June, 1993, the Reds appeared to give up, mis-passing the ball and hardly running. Crazy Calls staged a first in Japanese sporting history by cheering for the other side. This, one of them explained, was tough love, an education for their team: 'Supporters send a clear message in order to make the players function to their full capacity. Each of us is sometimes kind and sometimes harsh.'

Support with this kind of energy and focus did not just happen by itself. Japanese public behaviour is typically the opposite of the Reds supporters': people mind their manners and try not to attract attention. But the Japanese make up for this when they move into let-go mode. Office workers who put up with unreasonable bosses for long hours without uttering a word of complaint cast off their decorum after dark. With a few drinks inside them they are transformed into party animals, singing terrible *karaoke* and sprawling drunkenly along city streets. More than most other societies, appropriate behaviour in Japan depends on place and occasion, and the Japanese switch their inhibitions on or off accordingly.

To convert stadiums from public places where people were careful not to speak – let alone shout – out of turn, into settings for after-hours revelry, a new breed of crowd leaders grew up. They stood behind the goal, often on a step ladder or railings for extra height, and watched the flow of play. At crucial stages of the match – corners or free-kicks, or when one team launched a promising attack – they signalled to a drummer to start banging out a rhythm, and exhorted the crowd through a megaphone to chant or sing. Such leaders are alien to countries like Britain where there is a national antipathy to being told what to do. But they are active in other countries like Italy that have a tendency to form family-type groupings. Japanese supporters, too, preferred being led in a group. It created a framework for boisterousness, co-ordinated their efforts for maximum effect, and meant they were less likely to do anything wrong.

The effect of these leaders could be seen at any well-attended football match. When Japan played Peru in Yokohama on one occasion, tens of thousands of Japanese talked quietly among themselves as they lined up outside the stadium, mostly in their regular weekend dress of polo- or T-shirts with jeans or chinos. A few hundred Peruvians, nearly all wearing red and white team shirts, banged drums, waved flags and shouted, making far more noise than all the Japanese put together. The Peruvian support was going to murder the Japanese, right? Wrong. Once inside the stadium, the Japanese put on their blue replica shirts. Then, half an hour before kick-off, a drummer suddenly led a deafening chant of 'Ni-ppon! (da da da)'. They then kept this up for the full ninety minutes, without a break.

As well as this sharp divide between pre-match restraint and energetic support during a game, there were also hot and cold spots within a stadium. Football crowds in most countries have a hard core of fans, usually behind the goal, and the tension gradually tapers off towards the edges and in the side stands. In Japan there was no gradual tapering. The hard core could make as much noise as any crowd in the world, and generally had a fantastic time. But a few rows away, the other side of an invisible line, shouting and singing became as embarrassing as it would be in a shopping centre. These fans were purely spectators, and remained silent apart perhaps from clapping along with the drumbeat or gingerly slapping their thighs with a plastic megaphone. There were almost none of the in-between type of fan who sits alone, occasionally shouts some abuse or encouragement, and maybe joins in the odd chorus. It was all or nothing.

The leaders were crucial in determining the atmosphere at a Japanese football match, and each had his own ideas and style. Like most people in Kashima, Toru Kawazu had no particular interest in football as a child. His love was music, and as a teenager he died a blond streak in his hair and formed a punk band. Football first grabbed his attention when he noticed an affinity between the game and rock music. 'I read lots of music magazines, and musicians like Rod Stewart all mentioned in interviews how they liked football,' he recalled later. He had moved to Tokyo with his band to play clubs during a live music craze in the early nineties. But when this scene faded, and Kashima got a team in the new J.League, he went home to work in his parents' take-away meals business. He and the other band members learned as much as they could about the sport, and formed a supporters group called In.Fight. 'I watched football videos, and saw that the way fans behaved at matches had the same kind of feeling as punk rock,' he said. 'None of us were interested in football – we just liked standing up and making noise. The Japanese in general didn't like football. So we decided to make it fun.'

Zico had brought several Brazilian players and coaches to the Antlers, and Kawazu borrowed football videos from them. He adapted some chants and songs from these, and also sang the standard 'Ole, Ole, Ole, Ole! Oh-lay, Oh-lay!' Kawazu and his pals stood with megaphones at the front of the stands urging along the puzzled spectators, many of them middle-aged, all of them from the country. They ran up and down the stands chanting and singing to demonstrate. They banged drums and tried to start chants for individual players – 'Zi-co! (da da da)' – but still the crowd sat in silence. 'The Japanese personality was a big barrier,' he said. 'They are very shy and keep their emotions inside. They all smiled and said, "Thanks for telling us, we'll do it from now on." But they didn't. They were all too embarrassed.' After months of effort though, In.Fight convinced the quiet people of Kashima that it was OK to be noisy in football stadiums. After a year, boosted by the side's Zico-led rise in the league, most of the stadium was singing along with 'Ole, Ole, Ole, Ole! . . .' From twenty members at the outset, In.Fight would eventually grow to over 10,000.

Despite the early fervour, Kawazu and other leaders realised the danger of a drop-off in atmosphere as the J.League lost its novelty. In the first couple of years, crowds were featured in magazines and on TV, and football matches became something all trend-conscious Japanese – nearly the whole country, that is – had to sample. For Kawazu, the danger was free-riders: people enjoying the party mood but not contributing. Though he didn't call for a ban on women, he used media interviews and a column in the Antlers' fanzine to make it clear that only noisy people were welcome behind the goal. 'To secure a basic degree of passion you need rules behind the goal, which may mean normal people can't come near,' he explained. 'If people come along just to savour a bit of the atmosphere, then the level of excitement drops. So it's essential to have disadvantages to being behind the goal – like having to stand throughout the match, being squashed so you can hardly see, having things thrown at you, or getting into arguments. Then the only people there are those willing to put up with all this. If it's too comfortable, people will sit down at halftime or eat during the match, and the level of excitement will fall. That's why I always say, if you're not going to support, then don't come behind the goal.'

Other leaders relied on persuasion to keep the mood right. In Kashiwa, another medium-sized town outside Tokyo, Yoichi Yamamoto (no relation to the Flügels support leader) took over as Kashiwa Reysol supporters' leader amid a cooling mood on the club's crowded metal terraces. His predecessor had barked orders at the fans, who got sick of this and refused to join in his chants. Yamamoto, instantly recognisable for the white towel he wrapped round his head for matches, was more diplomatic. He gathered consensus at pre-match meetings with representatives from Reysol's several dozen supporters' groups. He insisted on some rules, like wearing yellow shirts to turn the home terrace into a solid wall of colour for maximum intimidation (the name Reysol combined the Spanish words for king – *rey* – and sun – *sol* – so the team wore sun-coloured uniform). But when some sections of the terrace had been slacking during a match, instead of scolding them, he loudly – and jokingly – shouted at a noisier section where he had close friends: 'You weren't trying much today, were you!' The ones who really hadn't been trying would hear this, reflect on their own lack of effort, and do better next time.

The result was that Kashiwa, despite being a small club, had one of the noisiest stands in the country. One of the lucky J.League teams to have a stadium with no running track, the terrace came to just four metres away from the goal-line, and was only separated from the pitch by a net to prevent stray balls flying out of the ground. When an away goalkeeper walked to the home end at the start of a half, the fans greeted him with a torrent of boos and whistles. Most opposing goalies stared at their feet until they had walked far enough to turn their back on the crowd. When the opposition got a penalty, Yamamoto beckoned fans forward with his megaphone. They rushed forward and climbed the net in front of the terrace, shrieking and pulling monkey faces to put off the penalty taker. They climbed the net too when Reysol scored, this time shaking it with hands and feet in riotous celebration. In summer they sometimes brought along a children's paddling pool, which they inflated inside the ground, and filled by carrying buckets of water from the toilets. Reysol goals were then celebrated by chucking water over the ecstatic crowd. Later, they got round a J.League ban on smoke bombs by building their own dry ice machine to spread carbon dioxide smoke after goals. Their most famous innovation was the '*Brief-tai*' – 'Briefs Corps', a group of about a dozen fans who lined up to salute the players before games wearing just white underpants.

The leader's job also came with responsibilities beyond creating a party mood. Most nastiness from Reysol's fans was of a good-humoured pantomime variety. When they booed the pre-match announcement of the opposition line-up, the sound was like that directed at the Ugly Sisters in a panto performance of *Cinderella*. Sometimes though, Yamamoto had to field complaints by people who thought the atmosphere was unwholesome. Among the targets were taunts aimed at opposing players, including '*Okusan to yatte yaru!*' – 'I'm going to fuck your wife'; a group of fans who held up a blow-up sex doll to put off the other team's penalty taker; and three supporters who dropped their trousers and underpants for the same purpose during a tie-breaking penalty shoot-out broadcast on national TV – two faced towards the pitch while one mooned. Another more gratuitous nude display came while a vast yellow, black and white Reysol banner was floated from the back of the terrace and down over the crowd before kick-off. Once, as it completed its passage and was gathered up at the front, two naked men were revealed facing the crowd. One did a version of the can-can using a small yellow flag and kicking with just his right leg: his leg hid his private parts when he high-kicked, then he deftly covered them with the flag as the leg came down. The other wore a peaked hat, and stood with his arms folded, staring straight ahead and hiding nothing. 'We were told this kind of thing was bad for children,' said Yamamoto. 'But I like being accused of behaving badly. It's more fun.'

However, Yamamoto took more seriously an obligation to prevent crowd violence. Because the organisation in the stands was so clear, mood creators like Yamamoto were automatically landed with a dual role as keepers of the peace. This contributed to the orderliness of Japanese crowds, and serious hooliganism was rare. After Reysol beat the Reds at the National Stadium, an exuberant Reysol fan shouted 'Come and have a go then!' at the upset Reds supporters, who outnumbered the Reysol fans about three to one. Even though the two groups of supporters were at opposite ends of a large stadium, so there was no possibility of the challenge being heard, Yamamoto rebuked the fan. 'And what do you think you're going to do if they do come over?' he asked through his megaphone so everyone else would hear too. The chastened supporter came over with an embarrassed smile and bowed his apologies. Yamamoto then returned to his normal, friendly manner: 'You can say what you like,' he laughed. 'But there are 20,000 of them and I'm not going to help you out!' There was relaxed chuckling all round, and a lesson had been learned. Said Yamamoto of his policy: 'I don't mind arguments as long as there's no violence and no one gets hurt. But I don't want to cross that line.'

As well as leaders' direct efforts to keep control, the loyalty they inspired acted as a further check on hooliganism. At one Urawa Reds match, a schoolboy was bragging loudly about a minor incident the week before: 'I was really pissed off, so I threw a plastic bottle.' Crazy Calls leader Koichi Yoshizawa had been called in by club officials and taken to task over this incident. So when a friend of Yoshizawa overheard the boast, he dressed the boy down with a lecture on his responsibilities: 'He's your leader! What's going to happen if you don't protect your leader?'

Sometimes a leader even accepted punishment on behalf of a crowd member. Kazuyoshi Miyazaki, leader of the Marinos support group *Kaizoku* – Pirates – did this in early 1996. The Marinos had lost five matches in a row, and an angry supporter threw a coin at a Flügels player during a Yokohama derby. Miyazaki, a shaggy-haired butcher with a charismatic blend of geniality and aggression, covered for the fan. He came forward to take responsibility, and accepted from club officials a personal ban from the stadium for the rest of that year.

The logic was the idea of group responsibility, something

encouraged in the Japanese from a young age. Examples include the annual high school baseball tournament, where a whole team is banned if anyone linked to it is caught breaking a rule, like smoking. In adult life, Japanese politicians and corporate heads regularly resign to take responsibility for misdemeanours occurring deep within their organisations, which they were not directly involved in. Group responsibility assumes that people feel worse about damaging their group and people they respect than they would about getting into trouble themselves. When this premise holds, it is a powerful incentive to good behaviour (though it can also be a way to sweep problems under the carpet so that things carry on like before). Miyazaki knew who had thrown the coin, and he thought the club officials probably knew, too. But he covered for the fan partly so the fan would not get in trouble, but mainly to show others the seriousness of the incident. This set an example to the rest of the supporters, and would make the club less likely to introduce crowd-control measures. It is likely the club played along because it thought Miyazaki's self-sacrifice would be the best way to prevent a repeat in the future. Without Miyazaki's leadership, the Marinos support flagged for the remainder of that year, and all the fans suffered from the drop-off in atmosphere. In fact, the coin thrower later appeared overly casual about the incident, something that annoyed other supporters and led to his estrangement from the main group. From the following year he stopped coming to Marinos games.

Crowd leading was exhausting work, and occasionally the pressure became too much. For the first two years of the J.League, Yoshizawa at the Reds was the most famous supporter in the land. Like club secretary Sato, he had watched the TV programme *Diamond Soccer* as a child, and loved the sound of what he thought were requiems in the grounds of England. Still a student when the J.League began, his powerful voice, charisma and imagination made him a natural boss for Crazy Calls. Fans with ideas for new chants suggested them to him, and he would add them to the repertoire if they were good enough (the signature Warrior cry came about like this). Standing at the front of terrace, black megaphone in hand and usually stripped to the waist, he read the state of the match, and called the shouts: a fast chant of 'Urawa Reds! Urawa Reds!' when they needed a goal; something more stately, like the chorus from Beethoven's ninth symphony, to maintain a winning position. As boss of the Urawa terraces, younger fans treated him like an elder brother, and when he arrived before a match, the crowd parted so he could take his place at the front. Eventually he became tired of the expectation that he would create a scene at every match – as well as the hazards of the job. In September 1995, he found himself in the same Korean barbecue restaurant as a defender he had abused from the stands through his megaphone. They started arguing, and the player dragged Yoshizawa outside and gave him a mild beating. Enough was enough. Yoshizawa resigned as leader to become a sports writer, and Crazy Calls split into groups like the 'Urawa Boys' and 'Dangerous Boys'.

Supporters could not always come up with their own ideas, as Kashima Antlers' Toru Kawazu explained: 'I really liked English-style support, with lots of singing, but I didn't want to just imitate what they were doing abroad. I thought the styles would be different from country to country – like the Koreans have their drums and the Arabs have that wailing sound. But the problem in Japan is the generation gap. Young people think older tunes are boring. And older people don't know any more recent songs.'

So Japanese fans did what European and South American crowds have done for decades: copy what they heard elsewhere. Though *Diamond Soccer* ended in 1988, the advent of satellite broadcasters provided a new source of ideas. One of these, *WOWOW*, showed matches from Italy's Serie A from 1991 to 1998. Scott Joplin's 'Entertainer' (the theme from *The Sting*), Purcell's trumpet voluntary, the Beatles' 'Yellow Submarine' and 'Ob La Di Ob La Da' – the tunes were all sung (without words) in Italy and later sung in Japan. As satellite TV expanded in the mid-1990s, Sky Television's Japanese service broadcast live English games. The Tokyo Ultras learned all the words to the English football anthem 'You'll Never Walk Alone'. After England's supporters used the theme from *The Great Escape* at their 1998 World Cup match against Argentina, supporters of Japan's national team and several clubs 'sang' it too. Marinos supporters saluted their – and Japan's – one-time captain Masami Ihara with 'I-ha-ra, I-ha-ra, I-ha-ra,' to the tune of the English standard 'Here we go'.

Support for football teams everywhere depends on some form of tribal feeling, and most leaders saw the paradox of serenading their local team with songs copied from the other side of the world. Of course, one attraction of football was that the game provided a link to other cultures, and Japanese crowds always contained a few people wearing Juventus, Manchester United or Inter Milan shirts. But this often went too far, and showed how hard it was for many Japanese to feel proud of their country. One problem was that national pride had gone to extremes in the past and ended up in nationalism and a disastrous war. Another was that decades of inhaling American culture had left some Japanese stuck with an idea that abroad was simply better. In any case, for the first year of the J.League, Yokohama Marinos fans chanted in Italian ('*Forza Marinos!*') and English ('We are Marinos!') and Spanish ('*Fuerza Marinos!*'). Then one of the Japanese players asked Pirates leader Miyazaki why they didn't support in their own language, as all the players were Japanese apart from three Argentines. After first checking with the team interpreter that this wouldn't offend the Argentines, Miyazaki changed the chants to the Japanese '*Gambare, Marinos!*' ('Go for it, Marinos!') and '*Yuke, Marinos!*' ('Go, Marinos!'). One fan told him Japanese chants were boring, but Miyazaki insisted. 'I am Japanese and love Japan,' he explained. 'But lots of Japanese don't. They think American things are cool and English is cool.'

On the other hand, Miyazaki was entranced by a vision of

near-bedlam in a TV documentary about Argentine football. At a match between Gimnasia de Jujuy and River Plate, enormous banners floated over a crowd of half-naked bodies jumping up and down like pogo sticks. Fans threw dozens of toilet rolls onto the pitch, as soldiers patrolled with German Shepherd dogs and automatic rifles. When underdog home team Gimnasia de Jujuy won the game, ecstatic fans swarmed onto the field and tore shirts, shorts and socks off their players for souvenirs. One carried the team captain round the pitch on his shoulders. After this Miyazaki attempted to lead the Marinos fans in Argentine-style support, twirling shirts over their heads, throwing streamers, and stretching red, white and blue strips of nylon down the stands. He got hold of videos of Boca Juniors and River Plate games and put Japanese lyrics to those fans' songs. He led a few pitch invasions, getting taken away in handcuffs on one occasion. And when Marinos won the J.League championship in 1995, he carried captain Ihara round the field on his shoulders.

Japan's football supporters thought so hard about how to create the right scene that they ended up with an ideology. Even if there was no Way of Football Support to follow, Japanese fans would make their own versions. If they were going to do it the Brazilian way, they would have a professional band – like Verdy – or take lessons from Brazilians – as S-Pulse's fans did. The Urawa Reds were the leading proponents of the other school of fandom – the boys' school, as practised in Italy (the banners), England (the songs) and Argentina (the confetti). Crazy Calls distilled this into a series of meditations and prescriptions published as *The Red Book*. According to this, in spite of doing something as Japanese as studying foreign techniques to improve their support, Crazy Calls thought of themselves as a breed apart from their countrymen. They had cast off Japan's usual social restraints – the shyness, the lack of spontaneity, the imperative not to offend – and become part of a world community of football fans who 'just go ahead and shout': 'Maybe we need to give up being

Japanese just a little. It is not easy to change from a mentality that dislikes confrontation to one that insists on its own point of view. Unfortunately, the red blood of the race of football supporters did not flow in our ancestors.'

Maybe not, but it flowed in 1990s Urawa, which became famous for the largest fan base in the country, and those fans' dogged loyalty to a team that never came close to winning anything – indeed was relegated to J2 the year after the J.League formed a second division. The crowd was usually as entertaining as the football, and just as intense: 'The twelfth players fighting behind the goal polish their minds and bodies,' said *The Red Book*. 'The growing seriousness becomes a manifesto, and echoes throughout the stadium. ... The red wave has moved.'

CHAPTER FIVE

Sparta

Like most Japanese boys growing up in the 1950s, Kunishige Kamamoto longed to be a baseball player. Baseball was the nation's number one sport, and Kamamoto dreamed of playing in the celebrated high school baseball championship, and then later in one of Japan's two professional leagues. Baseball, he thought, 'seemed glamorous, cool, strong and manly'.

Kamamoto played football, too, and when he was twelve and nearing the end of junior school, he was kicking a ball around one day after class, when the teacher who coached football asked him what sport he would play after moving on to junior high school. 'Baseball,' said Kamamoto.

'I see,' said the teacher. 'But you know, Kamamoto, with baseball, you can maybe make it to Koshien (the high school championship) and then play baseball for a college or company team. But pro baseball is really tough. And though baseball is really popular in Japan, the only other country they really play it in is America . . . Why don't you play football? Football is played all over the world. If you get good, you could even play in the Olympics.'

That last word persuaded him. It was just after the 1956 Melbourne Olympics, and Japan's twenty medal winners, mainly in gymnastics, swimming and wrestling, were national heroes. Kamamoto had recently started dreaming of going abroad, something that was difficult in those days for most ordinary Japanese, as they could not usually obtain passports for tourism. So with his sights set on the Olympics, he joined the junior high school football club.

It was miserable. The new boys were instructed to line up by the field, and shout '*Gambare!*' – 'Do your best!' – as the older boys played. When the older boys had shooting practice, the first years were told to stand behind the goal and pick up the stray balls – but were not allowed to kick them. With their own practice limited to twenty-kilometre runs, Kamamoto and a few friends decided baseball would be more fun. 'The kids playing baseball at the next ground were at least wearing gloves, and they could catch the balls as they flew out of the field,' he remembered later.

So Kamamoto stopped going to football practice, and Japan almost lost its top international goal scorer, whose record of seventy-three strikes in full internationals would remain unsurpassed into the twenty-first century. Luckily, however, an older boy who had been at the same junior school confronted him and asked him why he wasn't coming to training any more. Not daring to tell his senior that he planned to give up football, Kamamoto went back to running and picking up balls. At the same time, he started practising after school hours. He worked on lobs, trapping and shooting from passes – all things he was not allowed to do at junior high school. He also started kicking a stone on the thirty-minute walk to school.

When eventually allowed to kick the ball at school, Kamamoto was better than the other first years, and even some of the senior boys. At the school's summer training camp, he was the only first year, and the older boys used him as a servant. His days were a series of errands, and every sentence seemed to start with two words: one was his nickname, 'Gama'; the other was '*Oi*', a word used to beckon a subordinate. '*Oi*, Gama! Make sure the balls are pumped up before practice.' '*Oi*, Gama! Wipe the balls clean.' At night the older boys wrapped him in a futon, and then climbed on top of him till he could hardly breathe. 'They did what they liked,' he wrote in an autobiography, 'and you weren't allowed to resist. I wanted the camp to end as quickly as possible. But by this time, however hard the camp was, I never felt like giving up soccer. In my heart was always the idea of the Olympics and "the world".'

The same spirit kept him going through college. Waseda in Tokyo was one of Japan's top universities, and

Jump! Dettmar Cramer (*left*) directed Japan's leap from 'ping pong' football to Olympic bronze at Mexico '68.

Even at full stretch Gary Lineker found on-field success hard to come by in Japan. One newspaper calculated he was paid about £1 million per J.League goal.

Before the spit – Zico lets referee Shizuo Takada know what he thinks of the fateful penalty decision.

The 'Kazu dance': Kazuyoshi Miura was the
star of the J.League's early boom years.

Attention! Kashiwa Reysol fans salute their team in characteristic style.

(Facing page)
(Above) Happy? Dragan Stojkovic, here with Yasuyuki Moriyama (15),
taught Grampus players that losing was the direst misery but winning was
an unparalleled joy.

(Below) Brazil captain Dunga saw his role in Japan as an educator.
Here Takahiro Yamanishi (14) receives a lesson in Dunga's
'football classroom full of love'.

It doesn't feel any worse than this. Hans Ooft comforts captain Tetsuji Hashiratani after Japan's gut-wrenching exit from the USA '94 qualifiers.

And it doesn't get any better than this. 16 November 1997 – Masayuki Okano celebrates scoring the goal that put Japan into their first ever World Cup.

Get stuck in! Philippe Troussier shows national team players how to be more aggressive.

Hounded – Hidetoshi Nakata, seen here arriving home from Italy, hated having his picture taken but didn't have much choice.

also had one of the best football teams. When Kamamoto entered, the coach was Koichi Kudo, a stocky old man known for his cloth cap and no-nonsense attitude. Turning up for his first practice, Kamamoto introduced himself: 'I'm Kamamoto, *yoroshiku onegaishimasu*' – 'nice to meet you.' Kudo glanced up at him suspiciously, but didn't reply.

The students played a practice match, and after the whistle blew for the end, Kamamoto saw Kudo crouching in the middle of the pitch, picking up stones and putting them in his pocket. 'He's probably picking them up so the players don't get hurt,' thought Kamamoto. 'What a nice coach.'

He began to walk off the pitch, but was stopped by Kudo's shouting: 'Hey! Training isn't over yet! Now it's time for sprints.' Kudo ordered the students to run a series of dashes between the halfway line and the goal line. Kamamoto soon tired and started running slowly in last place. Then, 'I felt things hit my head and backside. I looked back and saw Kudo was taking the stones out of his pocket and throwing them at us.'

Waseda won the Emperor's Cup twice while Kamamoto was there, but while Kudo stopped throwing stones at him, he never praised him. After a while, Kudo became ill and was replaced. Just before he graduated, Kamamoto visited the old coach's home to say goodbye. Kudo, as ever, hardly acknowledged the student, and instead fired questions at him about whether he was training properly. By now, Kamamoto was an emerging star in Japanese football, and had been given glowing write-ups in newspapers.

'Coach,' he said. 'You didn't praise me once in four years . . . '

'Don't be so stupid,' the old man replied. 'If I praised you that would be the end. You're young and have a future – that's why I get angry with you. The time you spend worrying about not being praised is time you should spend thinking about football.'

After graduating from Waseda, Kamamoto joined Yanmar Diesel Engine Co., which had a football team in the JSL. One day, the Yanmar coach showed him a letter he had received. It was from Kudo. Years later, just one passage remained in Kamamoto's memory: ' . . . if he moans or says he's tired, throw cold water over his head . . .'

There was a point to all this hardship. Though the advent of the J.League turned football into a symbol of a more liberal Japan, it had previously been taught with the same grim ethos as every other sport there. Sport in Japan was not about playing games or having fun, but was a tool of education. It taught children about obedience and hierarchy in an organisation, as well as how to withstand the pain of long training sessions. This made sport the ideal preparation for life working in a Japanese company, which highly valued the ability to work well in a group, accept strict hierarchy and tolerate punishing work hours. More than brains and learning, recruiters always looked for graduating students who had been active in college sports clubs.

Thirty years later, little had changed in some Japanese schools, as Shoji Jo, another future international striker, discovered. Jo was a star striker at the age of fifteen, and several high school coaches asked him to come to their school. One of these was Takashi Matsuzawa of Kagoshima Vocational High School in Kyushu, the southernmost of Japan's four main islands. Matsuzawa visited Jo's house several times, and called him on the telephone to tell him how much the school wanted him. Jo, however, wasn't interested. He knew that players in the school's football club were all made to cut their hair extremely short.

Most Japanese school sports clubs insisted on short-cropped hair. Though the definitions were loose, there were roughly three grades of school haircut: *sports-gari* – sports crop, a bit like a crew-cut; *bozu* – monk cut, a short version of a buzz cut; and *hage* – completely bald. Jo went to school in the days before head shaving became fashionable, and he had always liked to grow his hair. When he was a toddler, he even had an Afro-style perm with a ribbon tied in it. At school, however, he had been forced to crop his hair to about *bozu* level, and by the end of junior high school was sick of this. So instead of Kagoshima Vocational, he was considering going to one of the other top football high schools, where more generous-spirited coaches allowed their charges to wear relatively long sports crops. Then coach Matsuzawa told him: 'By the time you come, I'm going to allow boys to grow their hair.' Matsuzawa also promised that he could wear a number 9 shirt with his name on it. That was enough for Jo, and he decided to go to Kagoshima Vocational.

But a month after he joined the school, Matsuzawa ordered him to go *bozu*. An older boy at the school explained to him: 'He makes those phone calls every year. I had the same thing.' Jo realised he had been duped, but it was too late to change – and he didn't know how bad things would get.

Because the school was too far from his home to commute daily, Jo lived with nine other boys in a ten-*tatami*-mat (roughly twenty-square metre) room on the second floor of the coach's house. They studied and slept there, and were allowed nothing but a television for amusement. But Jo's parents had sent him a Nintendo Entertainment System as a present, and the boys hid it in a gap behind the TV. When all was quiet on the ground floor, they crawled off their futons, and held Nintendo competitions. 'We were playing football all day at school,' Jo remembered, 'and the Nintendo was a good way to relieve stress. It sounds sad that sixteen-year-olds had nothing to enjoy but a Nintendo system, but we had almost no free time, and because we were all either *bozu* or bald, we didn't have much chance with girls.'

One night, the Nintendo was missing. 'Shoji, you're going to be in trouble tomorrow,' one of the other boys warned, and Jo couldn't sleep that night, thinking about what would happen. The next day, the coach summoned him: 'You! What's this toy? Go and shave your head!'

Another shaving came after Jo's skills and pretty-boy looks made him popular with girls. In his first year at Kagoshima Vocational, the school qualified for the national championships, and as a rare first-year regular on the team, Jo attracted some media attention. He started getting fan letters, and by his second year, about twenty or thirty such letters had arrived at the coach's house. Matsuzawa summoned Jo again: 'You! How many girls have you got?'

'I don't know,' replied Jo, because he didn't know how many girl fans he had.

And the order came again: 'Go and shave your head!'

First he was close-cropped with clippers, and then polished off with a razor. 'You look like a criminal!' the coach laughed afterwards, and took mug-shot photos of him from the front, back and sides.

In his third year, Jo became team captain, and the frequency of shavings increased. He was responsible for things like making sure the boys' room was clean. But he was not strict with his juniors, and the coach made him take responsibility for the slackness under his watch. The punishment was always baldness, and if his head wasn't completely smooth, the coach got out a razor and finished off the job. In his first and second years, Jo had to shave his head four or five times for his own misdemeanours. In his third year, he was shaved three times to take responsibility for the group as a whole. 'For me, this was always the biggest humiliation,' he wrote later in an autobiography. 'I thought the coach knew the thing I hated the most, because I had basically decided to go to Kagoshima Vocational after being told it would be OK to grow my hair. Each time I was made to get my head shaved, my naïve, pure heart was wounded a little.'

Jo's experiences were not unusual, and young Japanese footballers put up with this treatment because high school sport was a big deal. Though the J.League ushered in a new era, high school football was for years the pinnacle of the game. The final of the national high school championship often sold out the 50,000-seat National Stadium, which was almost always more than the Emperor's Cup final attracted, and far more than any JSL match. It was taken so seriously that coaches scouted junior high school teams to entice the best players, and many boys like Jo lived away from home either in dormitories or small apartments just so they could go to a high school with a top football team.

Japan's most successful high school football coach was Sadao Konuma of Teikyo High School in northwest Tokyo. A thick-set man, who kept himself in shape with pre-dawn runs, he joined Teikyo in 1964. After taking over the football club the following year, he led the school to a record six national championships, as well as numerous second and third places, which were commemorated by gold, silver and bronze footballs displayed in a trophy cabinet in the school entrance hall.

He had succeeded through a combination of old-fashioned control and modern innovation. His starting point was a football version of 'management baseball', which he defined as telling people 'what they must not do, what is unacceptable, and in a way regulating their freedom or controlling them, training players by rules – a system to bind them.' Though he claimed not to be especially rough, he acknowledged that his methods could be described as Spartan. If they didn't listen to his first warning, he told them, 'Learn from the pain of my knuckles!' and hit them. 'My principle is that football means nurturing human beings,' he wrote in a 1983 book on his educational principles. 'In the framework of management football, boys turn into youths and youths into adults.'

Teikyo High School had appeared to need some sorting out when Konuma first arrived. Turning up to a job interview, a group of boys hanging around near the entrance to the school saw him, a young adult, and demanded: 'Give us a cigarette.' Another boy simply advised him not to come to teach at the school. Later he heard horror stories from other teachers. Many kids at the school could not read the newspaper or even simple place names – shocking in a country with one of the world's highest rates of literacy. One cold day, when a classroom stove ran out of coal, a group of boys had simply broken up some desks and chairs to use for kindling. Another time, a teacher who caught a boy cheating in an exam later went to check up on the boy. '*Urusei!*' – 'Piss off!' the boy shouted back, and pulled a knife out of his bag.

Konuma therefore felt that a tough line was necessary. To ensure no one complained about his methods, at the beginning of each school year Konuma gathered the parents of boys wanting to join the football club, and explained how he ran things: 'I don't hit players because they are no good at football. I won't kill or injure a child. But I believe that improving a person makes him better at football. So if a student starts doing wrong, even if it is unrelated to football, I will shout at him. If he doesn't understand, I will hit him mercilessly. Hitting is considered unreasonable in society at large, but in this world it is sometimes necessary. So I believe in *ai no muchi* – tough love (literally "the whip of love"). If this is all right by you, please let me look after your child. I will do so responsibly.' To the boys themselves, he warned that his club was not somewhere just to keep fit or to make friends. Moreover, he told them, they would not kick a ball for the first three months.

Every spring over fifty new boys asked to join the school football club, with up to 100 applying some years. With boys from all three years of high school, this would add up to a total of 150 or 200 at any one time, way too many for the available space. What's more, Konuma didn't like not being able to keep a close eye on so many boys – they might be misbehaving out of his sight. But his intimidating introductory talks normally did the trick and the number of boys who wanted to join normally declined to about thirty. When these actually started the club activities – running, wiping the balls clean and tending the practice ground – the dropouts mounted. 'More than a way to raise their basic level of fitness,' wrote Konuma, 'the three months of just running is a way to see how obedient they are, and how much patience they have.' This final cull normally resulted in a club numbering seventy or eighty boys spread over three years.

Konuma made sure the survivors behaved themselves. He hit them for possessing cigarettes, for skipping practice to get a motorbike licence and for skipping class and going home early. Other punishments included the ubiquitous head shaving – for boys whose hair was too long – and cleaning the school toilets. After a while, Konuma's reputation was enough to keep the boys quiet, and in later years he guessed he was only hitting boys about once a year. But, 'when I was young, I used my hand before my mouth . . . and my fist used to be swollen from punching them so much,' he wrote. 'Admonishment is education and hitting is education. Even if the means is different, the aim of correcting the students is the same. But I am not good at arguing verbally why things are right and wrong – like why cigarettes are OK for adults but not for schoolboys.'

His harshest discipline was directed at older boys who beat up younger ones. He sometimes punished such groups of older boys by making them sit on the pitch in a manner called *seiza*. This is a formal position used in polite company, where you sit on the ground with the lower legs folded under the thighs. This means the feet are tucked uncomfortably under the buttocks, soles upwards. The ankles take most of the body weight, and it soon becomes painful. Lining them up like this, he then hit them in turn – so hard on one occasion that he broke his hand.

Apart from maintaining discipline, Konuma's main message to his young players was that they must win, and that winning needed hard training and *konjo* – 'guts' or 'fighting spirit'. Every year he developed the boys by pushing them to the limit of their endurance, and then getting them to go a little further. During term the football club shared the school's only practice area, an earth pitch about seventy metres on each side, with the baseball club (a smaller rugby club sometimes practised on a rooftop). So that the football club could have the pitch to itself, he instituted 7 a.m. training sessions, before lessons started at 8.30 a.m. For players who lived two hours away by train, that meant getting up as early as 4.30 a.m. At summer camps, he allowed players just four or five hours sleep a night, before making them train under a burning summer sun till they could no longer stand. If a player fell over exhausted, he threw water over him to make him get up. Some players didn't get up even then, but Konuma thought half of these were just playing dead because they wanted to rest. So he tested them. He pulled down their shorts, and if they were genuinely exhausted they still would not move. But if they were only pretending, they would jump up with embarrassment and cover themselves, and Konuma would say: 'Look at you! You're still fine!' Worn out by this regime, some boys quit in the middle of the camp. But a few others still had enough energy to make a noise after lights-out, and to these, Konuma yelled, 'Get outside!' and made them do sit-ups under the stars for an hour.

Sometimes Konuma, troubled by a moment of introspection, worried that he frightened the boys too much. While some left the football club, others lived in fear of him – so much so that they were afraid to ask to attend to basic physical needs. He once saw a boy on the field squirming, and noticed after a while that he was leaking something from his shorts. 'What's up?' Konuma asked him.

'Sir . . . the toilet . . .'

'Oh, I see. Well, go on, then.'

'I've already gone,' replied the boy.

Konuma was driven by a belief in sport as a corrective to bad behaviour, and felt he was on a mission to provide children with fundamental life skills through football. He made personal sacrifices, at first receiving little thanks. Because of the limited school budget, he spent a lot of his own money on things like balls and lime to mark out the pitch. He took practice from seven each morning, was at the ground till seven or eight in the evening, and caught up on deskwork in the staff room till eleven at night. But when he started early-morning training, the head teacher complained that he didn't want the boys falling asleep during lessons, and other teachers complained that the football club members didn't study properly. When he was seen eating a roll in the street, because he didn't have time to eat a proper breakfast, the lapse in manners cost him points on his job appraisal.

He summed up his method as '*ame to muchi*' – 'candy and whip', the Japanese equivalent of carrot and stick – and often bought boys a soft drink or a bowl of noodles when they came to his house to apologise for misbehaviour. When one boy, who Konuma referred to as K, committed some bad behaviour that Konuma chose not to specify, he threw him out of the football club. K came to the staff room to apologise: 'I will never do anything bad again. Please forgive me, *sensei*.' Konuma didn't believe the boy was truly sorry, however, so sent him away.

K began a campaign for reinstatement. He waited outside Konuma's house early in the morning when the teacher would be leaving for work, and again late at night when he was coming home, and apologised again, pleading: 'I was a bad member of the club. I regret what I did. I don't have anything else but football.' At first Konuma continued to repel him. But eventually he decided the boy was sincere, and let him back in the club, where he became a key member of the team. 'If I had immediately let him back,' reflected Konuma, 'he would not have changed his thinking and would not have done so well later. He would probably have only gone half-way as a human being. And if I had never let him back, I'm sure he would have dropped out. It is hard to tell when to crack the whip and when to give them candy, but you have to judge this from a boy's face.' He made sure there was more whip than candy, however, and estimated he doled them out in a candy:whip ratio of 3:7 or 2:8.

Other coaches had formidable reputations too. One such

was Yoshinori Shiwa, a barrel-chested man with a booming parade-ground voice, who coached Higashi Fukuoka High School to an unprecedented treble of high school titles in 1997: the national high school championship; the all-Japan youth championship; and the football competition in the national physical education championships. As well as regularly hitting and kicking students, he once turned the school staff room into what he described as a 'sea of blood'. Walking into the staff room one day, he heard a teacher telling off a second-year member of the football club. 'Hey, what have you done?' he asked the boy.

The boy said nothing.

'*Sensei*,' said Shiwa to the teacher. 'What has he done?'

'This boy hasn't come to school for over a week,' the teacher said. 'I was asking him why not.'

'That can't be true,' said Shiwa. 'He's been coming to training every day.'

He turned to the boy. '*Oi!* What are you up to?'

'I was just coming to training,' said the boy.

Like all Japan's high school coaches, Shiwa was an educator before he was a coach, and had always told his boys that a condition for membership of the football club was that they also be good students. He had thought highly of this particular boy, and had even been planning to make him the next team captain. Now he felt his trust had been betrayed, and he was angry.

He made the boy kneel in the *seiza* position, and began shouting. 'Who said you could only come to school to play football!' he yelled, and started hitting him. He hit him so hard that the force of the blow knocked the boy to the ground. So he held the boy still, and kicked him and hit him round the face. The boy's nose bled, and then blood started flowing from his mouth. His face turned red with blood, and soon the area around the boy was spattered red. The other teachers were too frightened of Shiwa's rage to stop him, but eventually the school judo coach, who had been alarmed by the noise, came over and pinioned him.

'Shiwa-*sensei*,' he said. 'Calm down. Don't you think that's enough?'

The 'sea of blood' incident turned Shiwa into a figure of fear, and in one way his job became much easier: he had no disciplinary problems in the health education lessons he taught, and the students all listened to him quietly. The only downside was that they ran away when they saw his face. Even when they had to talk to him, they kept their distance out of fear that he might hit or kick them: 'Even if I told them to come closer, they wouldn't. So I would take a step towards them, and they would take a step back.'

Amazingly, Konuma and Shiwa had both considered themselves to be relatively progressive, and they were convinced it was all for the boys' ultimate good. The boy Shiwa beat bloody stayed in the football club till graduation, and later went on to become deputy chairman of the football club old boys' association, as well as managing director of a company.

Japan's school coaches mellowed in later years, as corporal punishment became less acceptable, and as individual coaches like Konuma and Shiwa learned to use persuasion rather than physical means to correct boys' behaviour. 'Maybe I overdid it,' Shiwa admitted later in a memoir. 'But at the time I was hitting and kicking boys every day, so I didn't have the capacity to think of this . . . I was immature.'

They were also looking for new ways to improve their teams, and most began to discard the more extreme elements of their regimes as counterproductive. Instead of Sparta, they began to look to modern Europe and South America for ideas. Konuma was the first to take his team on an overseas tour – to West Germany in 1977. He later took his boys to South America every two years, first to Brazil, and then to Peru and Uruguay, where he could get better value for money. Students' families paid about 500,000 yen (around £2,000) per trip, which covered travel, lodging and instruction by a local coach for about one month. 'When we won the championship, it was written about in football magazines that we had improved by going to train in South America,' Konuma said. 'We became a model for others.' By the 1990s, about thirty or forty Japanese high schools regularly went on this kind of overseas football tour.

In another innovative move, Shiwa at Higashi Fukuoka tried to root out the hierarchy enforced by older players. During one summer training camp, most of the first years quit and went home. Shiwa initially thought he must have been imposing excessively hard training on the boys. But when he asked them, the problem turned out to be bullying. The seniors had been giving the first years a hard time when they made mistakes on the pitch, and imposing penalty runs of one lap of the field or a series of 100-metre dashes. Beyond that, they were also making the juniors do their washing and run other personal errands for them. The younger boys reluctantly obeyed their elders till they could stand it no longer. This custom had existed throughout the Japanese sports world – both amateur and professional – for years. Just about any Japanese sports team, office or institution had similar internal rules, and in addition to the errands, younger members had to use polite language to the elders to reinforce the hierarchy.

So Shiwa banned older boys from using first years for personal errands, and ordered moderation in penalty runs for mistakes. The traditional hierarchical system still remained intact, but absolute obedience was no longer required. Despite these reforms, most of the first years did not return to the club. Only four remained, and they were still bullied, though not as badly.

After this, Shiwa gradually reformed the football club. As at most schools, first-year students had been obliged to shout out encouragement during the seniors' shooting practice however tired they were and whether or not they really cared. There was also an irritating custom of forced politeness that everyone felt they had to obey. When an older boy, coach or other senior person came along, the first club member to spot him would shout out a greeting, like '*Ohayo gozaimasu*!' – 'Good morning!' This then started a chain reaction, as first the boys standing nearby repeated the greeting, and then those further away took it up. 'They are not seriously listening to and understanding what someone says,' thought Shiwa. 'They are only seriously replying to this.'

So he abolished or toned down all of these practices, and also reformed his training methods. Between 1988 and 1993, Higashi Fukuoka failed to qualify for the national championships, and Shiwa became obsessed with winning. He started dreaming of upcoming matches, and his wife complained of him talking in his sleep. In an effort to improve the team, he crammed as many different training exercises as possible into the available time, but felt that even this was not enough. The players became tired and lost their enthusiasm for training the next day. They couldn't concentrate properly and weren't learning from the practice. Even when they did learn an exercise, they often merely learned to carry it out in training, and couldn't apply their new skills in real matches. 'I would have understood this if I had thought about it coolly,' Shiwa reflected. 'But I hadn't realised, because I had thought that the only way to raise them all to the same level was through the time and quantity of practice.'

Shiwa decided to place the emphasis on ball skills first, tactics second, and relegate physical training to the third priority. Apart from a few warm-up routines, he abolished running without the ball and ended morning training. Instead of having to warm up together in a group, he allowed players to turn up whenever they had finished lessons and start kicking balls around by themselves. His new training sessions lasted only about ninety minutes, and also included free training. Japanese schools had been good at pushing children to reach a similar basic level of ability. But a consensus was developing that the nation needed to encourage individuals to work on their strong points and excel at whatever they could. Shiwa followed this new thinking on the football field, and allotted time for players to work on whatever they needed to: defenders on clearances and attacking players on shooting and build-ups.

Despite the toning down of boot camp regimes in schools football and the more flexible approach to training, there was still one main difference between Japan and the established football world. Even though the J.League required members to set up youth teams, the typical route to a professional contract at the turn of the century was still via high schools rather than a European-style apprentice system. This meant that a good but not outstanding young player, with dreams but no real prospect of making a living from football, still had a high school education to fall back on. The ultimate aim of almost all Japanese high school coaches remained the nurture of well-behaved members of society – with football forming a part of education rather than taking its place.

Whenever Konuma took Teikyo squads abroad, the overseas coaches were surprised by how polite and well behaved the boys were, and how carefully they listened to the instruction. His trips to South America convinced him that too much emphasis on football was a bad thing, because people there seemed to forget about everything but football. Instead of working to improve themselves, people there went to football matches, waved their shirts around their heads, and tried to forget about their lives. 'They forget about economics and politics and just think about football and who's won,' he said. 'I worry that kids will not be prepared for life if they can't making a living as professionals. We have to make them study and learn about life too.'

One Saturday in 2001 before the school term had started, a group of boys were running a series of short sprints in preparation for a practice match the following day. When a visitor arrived to talk to Konuma, they paused at the end of a dash, bowed and said, '*Ohayo gozaimasu!*' – 'Good morning!' After practice, a group of boys were washing the van that would take them to the next day's match: 'That van's already clean!' Konuma called out to them. 'You don't need to wash it again!' As he drove out of the school, the boys waited at the gate, where they bowed to him. 'There is a saying for martial arts like judo and kendo,' he explained. '"*Rei ni hajimete, rei ni owaru*" – "Start with a salutation, end with a salutation." Football is from England and is not a martial art, but manners are still very important. If a player is good in terms of skill and tactics but his manners are bad, he is a bad sportsman. It's about education rather than football. All Japanese coaches teach this. This is more important than winning.'

CHAPTER SIX
Mind Games

After two years of the J.League, Nagoya Grampus badly needed a lift. Despite the money they'd spent on Gary Lineker, they came ninth and eighth out of ten teams in 1993. The next year, despite the addition of brilliant Yugoslav playmaker Dragan Stojkovic, the league's expansion to twelve afforded them the opportunity to finish even lower: eighth and then twelfth. Looking for a good manager to wake the team up, Grampus asked Guus Hiddink, who later coached the Dutch national team, Real Madrid and South Korea. But one visit to a match with Grampus at their nadir was enough to put him off, and he turned down the offer.

Arsène Wenger was Grampus' next choice for the job. He had spent a successful period of seven years at AS Monaco when they twice won the French championship. But by 1994, Wenger was going stale and Monaco were in a slump. Forced to quit, he planned to work as a FIFA technical coach in the United Arab Emirates. But a visit to Nagoya, when he was lucky enough to see Lineker's last game, persuaded him otherwise. 'Even though Grampus were in last place, a position where it is difficult to maintain motivation, the players seemed to keep up their concentration to the end,' he wrote later in a book published in Japan. 'The fans were different from those in Europe – they were quieter and did not hurl abuse at opposing players.'

Arriving to try to save this desperate outfit, Wenger initially flopped. The first problem was the old confidence issue. Nagoya had just finished bottom of the J.League, and, noticed Wenger, 'the Grampus players did not have the experience of winning, so they had forgotten the hope that their team could win.' So he gave the players simple exercises, and put them through gruelling physical work-outs: while the running and weight training would toughen the players' bodies, tasks they could perform adequately would boost their confidence and toughen their minds. But over Wenger's first three months, the team just got worse. The players seemed even more aimless and unmotivated than before, and lost eight out of their first ten games, putting them bottom of the fourteen teams that now made up the league. After the last of these – a 4–0 defeat to the Antlers – Wenger could no longer stand his players' negative attitude. 'What are you afraid of?' he yelled at them in disgust. 'Can you call yourselves professionals playing like this?'

Wenger eventually realised that the problem was not skill, tactics, or even just a simple confidence issue, but something much deeper. 'There was a wall between me and the Grampus players,' he wrote. 'The know-how I had developed in Europe was of no use with this wall.' Specifically, when players got the ball during training, they would often hesitate, waiting for the foreign master-coach to prompt their next move. 'They wanted specific instructions from me. But football is not American football, where the coach can give instructions for each play over headphones. The player with the ball should be in charge of the game. I had to teach them to think for themselves.'

That's the way it was with many of the more than sixty foreign managers who coached in the first decade of the J.League. They were brought to Japan to pass on their knowledge of skills and tactics, but sometimes found their biggest task was dealing with the mental aspect of the game. In the worst cases they found players had been drained of self-confidence and trained not to take the initiative. 'The history of Japanese sport shows that everything is adjusted to the traditional Japanese way of thinking with lots of coach control,' said Yoichi Kozuma, a sport psychologist at Tokai University near Tokyo. 'So although we imported a lot of ideas and practice methods – strategy, technique and skills – the big problem was that many Japanese coaches were only interested in skill and strategy. They didn't learn about how to coach and motivate.'

Stuart Baxter was better prepared than most for Japan. He had grown up in Birmingham as the son of Bill Baxter, a coach at Aston Villa in the 1960s. Because of his father's job, Baxter was sometimes bullied by the city's anti-Villa element. At first he was just pushed around and made fun of, but one day four or five older boys beat him up and broke his nose. He decided to learn to defend himself properly, and began to study karate. After playing as a defender for clubs including Preston North End, Stockport County and Dundee, Baxter moved to Sweden in the middle of his playing career, and ended up managing Halmstads BK. When they won the second division title in 1989, Baxter told a press conference that he thought team harmony and mental balance were very important for a team. He explained about his karate studies, and mentioned that he often read about Zen and eastern culture. The next day's papers featured him under the headline: 'English manager with Japanese spirit'.

But even Baxter's karate and Zen studies did not prepare him fully to deal with Japan. When the Mazda team went on a post-season tour of Europe, Halmstads BK played a friendly match against them, and Baxter got to know the club's general manager Kazuo Imanishi. As Mazda morphed into Hiroshima Sanfrecce for the J.League, Imanishi asked Baxter to manage the team. Joining Sanfrecce in 1992, he at first came across to the players as bad-tempered, so much so that the club interpreter felt the need to soften his language. After one match Sanfrecce lost at home, he said: 'We would have won today's game if it wasn't for stupid mistakes.' But instead of the Japanese word for 'stupid' – *bakageta* – the interpreter translated this as *tsumaranai* – more like 'tedious'. Baxter understood some Japanese and told off the interpreter for diluting his message.

For their part, the Japanese players expressed themselves far less directly than he was used to in Europe. 'In other countries,' he said, 'if you drop a player they'll come and batter your door down and it's "Why aren't you fucking picking me?" In Japan, they come and say, "Mr Baxter, can I do anything to improve my game? I feel I'm not doing well enough." It was important for me to learn that mental game so I could tell when they were angry without having the conflict.'

So Baxter decided to find out what made the players tick, and got them all to write down the most important things to them as professional footballers. Most answers consisted of things like 'winning' and 'playing in matches'. From these and conversations with the players, he decided they were full of anxiety over the possibility of failure. Instead of wanting to win, they felt they had to win, and worried about the consequences of losing.

When Japanese players made a mistake during a match, they often turned to their teammates and said, "*Gomen nasai*" – "Sorry." Then after the game they told the coach and everyone else who wanted to hear: 'It's no good. I played terribly today.' Baxter thought this was rooted in players' fear of displeasing the boss. One player told him about his relationship with a coach he had played for previously: 'It was not very friendly. When the coach laughed, I had to laugh too, even if something wasn't funny. I was very uneasy.'

Japanese players were not, however, keen to admit to these anxieties. Baxter often saw them looking tense before games, and would ask them whether they were nervous or if they were worried about anything else. But the answer was always, '*Daijobu*' – 'I'm OK', even when they were clearly not feeling OK. Baxter resolved to change these negative thoughts in their minds to more positive orientations.

One player requiring such nurturing was Hajime Moriyasu, a defensive midfielder. Baxter thought he was good, because he made brave, well-timed tackles. Hans Ooft thought he was good, too, and called him up to play for the national team. But not everyone was in the Moriyasu fan club: Moriyasu himself didn't think he was much good.

Returning from an injury in the 1994 first stage, Moriyasu's form took a dive, and he got into a vicious spiral of feeling frustrated with himself, not wanting to make mistakes, and then actually making more mistakes, and told Baxter after matches: '*Kantoku* – manager, I'm sorry.' Baxter put an arm round his shoulders and gave him some fatherly encouragement. 'You don't have to say that,' he said. 'You did your best, didn't you? And next time will be even better.'

Baxter decided to ignore Moriyasu's mistakes, and make comments only when he did something good, like an effective pass. When he substituted him, Baxter told him: 'You've improved.' In training most days he said to him, 'You're better than you were yesterday, aren't you?' In one talk Baxter said: 'Don't worry. Even great players make mistakes. The problem is when good players worry too much about making mistakes, they get nervous and then make a series of mistakes. The better a player is, the more those around him demand from him.'

The art of subtle communication was also needed to deal with club management. Baxter made one early mistake at the beginning of the 1994 season, when general manager Imanishi wanted to talk about arrangements for the following year. Baxter was used to these things being decided at the end of a season, and couldn't understand why Imanishi was bringing it up so early. So he pointed out what he thought was an obvious principle – that his job prospects depended on his performance – but with a little too much western bluntness. 'If I have a nightmare, you'll sack me,' he said. 'And if I do well and get an offer for three or four times as much, then I'll take it.'

Imanishi took this to mean Baxter would be leaving, and lined up another coach for 1995. Sanfrecce won the first-stage championship that year, which was an extraordinary achievement for an unfancied team with none of the big-name stars at clubs like Verdy, Antlers and Marinos. The club would probably have liked to keep Baxter on, but could no longer get out of its new deal. Baxter had to move on. 'It was wrong of me,' he reflected several years later. 'Imanishi wouldn't have sacked me – he would have just said that they needed another coach. And I would have liked to have followed up, but we both misunderstood each other because of the earlier conversation.'

But by the end of his stay in Japan, Baxter had transformed himself into a skilled reader of the Japanese mind. He left Hiroshima on good terms, and Imanishi even helped him get a new job with Vissel Kobe, who were still in the Japan Football League, one step lower, and seeking entry to the J.League.

When Baxter dropped Vissel's captain for one game, he had a feeling the decision would be controversial. His fears were confirmed that evening at a club reception, when the chairman's assistant said the chairman wanted to have dinner with him afterwards. Baxter knew this meant the chairman wanted to complain about the captain being left out, so he explained that he was busy and could not make dinner. Not taking no for an answer, the chairman himself then came over to invite him for just a cup of coffee. 'That is very considerate of you,' replied Baxter. 'But I have to go home as soon as possible because it's my wife's birthday.'

Those words were enough to seal the issue, and the chairman got the message that Baxter wanted no interference in picking the team. Describing the incident later, he said: 'Anywhere else, and I would have said, "Piss off, and don't tell me how to pick the fucking team." Then he would have thrown a team sheet at me and given me an ultimatum. But in Japan I thought, I have to pay this guy some respect. So instead of that, we came to an agreement like this that I didn't want him interfering.'

The chairman's assistant gave him a lift home after the reception, and Baxter could see him smiling in the rear-view mirror. 'You knew what he wanted,' said the assistant. 'You're getting more Japanese than the Japanese.'

Besides confidence, another big issue for Japanese players was taking initiative on the field. This, too, was not always helped by strict coaching in schools. In his early days at Teikyo High, Konuma thought smart, wilful boys were not suited to sport, as they made poor team players and were potentially insubordinate. 'My method of instruction is authoritarian,' he wrote in his 1983 book. 'I say, "Do as I say, and you will win." This makes it hard when a know-all comes along. Team sports need the kind of stupidly obedient person who if they're told to turn right, they turn right. If the coach says, "This is white," then even if it is black, they believe it is white.'

While encouraging team discipline, this did not always make for imaginative players. Zico was immediately impressed by Japanese players' ability to study: they were the quickest learners he had ever come across, and in terms of effort to learn from an instructor he thought they were 'perhaps the best in the world'. But sometimes this earnestness went too far. In his early days with the Antlers, some players wrote down every word he said in notebooks, from basic advice during training to post-match assessments of what had gone right and wrong. Then, five minutes before the next match kicked off, they took out these notes and started revising. Zico, when he saw this, 'went beyond surprise and was completely dumbfounded'.

When Dutchman Frans van Balkom coached at Yomiuri Club in the early 1970s, he noticed before a practice game that the touchlines had worn thin. One of the players spoke some English, so van Balkom told him: 'Get the others to mark the lines.' Then he turned away and carried on talking to his assistant coach. After a while, van Balkom looked back, and saw the players hadn't done anything yet. 'Hey!' he shouted. 'The game starts in twenty minutes! Tell them to mark the lines. Do they think they're too good to do that?' The next time he looked, the players were all standing around the edge of the field about twenty meters apart in straight lines – what the English speaker had thought was marking the lines. 'If he didn't understand,' said van Balkom later, 'he could simply have asked, "What do you mean?" But he didn't want to ask me.'

When Ossie Ardiles went to manage Shimizu S-Pulse after a career in Argentina and England, he once told a defender to keep his hand on the near post for a corner: then he could maintain his position and cover the post. But when the corner went out to the edge of the other side of the penalty area, the player stayed right by his post with his hand on it, even though there was no longer any danger there. 'I had just meant him to touch the post as a way to know where he was,' said Ardiles.

They sometimes also stuck doggedly to instructions even after their relevance had passed. In 2000, after the J.League added a second division, Consadore Sapporo were easily the best team in the division, and Omiya Ardija had lost their first three matches to them that season. In the fourth, they decided to slow down the play to stop Sapporo taking an early lead, and the Omiya goalkeeper followed directions to take as much time as possible at each goal kick. But even after Sapporo opened the scoring after twenty-two minutes, the Omiya goalie continued wasting time. Omiya had an English player and a Dutch player, and they started remonstrating with him. But the goalkeeper had been given his instructions and wouldn't listen. So the two foreigners approached Leslie Mottram, a Scottish referee then employed by the J.League, and pleaded with him in vain to help them out. 'Can't you give him a yellow card?' they implored. 'He's taking too long over his goal kicks.'

When Wenger arrived at Grampus the players were at first unimpressed. A year previously, the club had followed Lineker's recommendation and called in Gordon Milne, his old mentor from Leicester City. But Milne's spell in Nagoya ended after less than a year, with Grampus bottom of the league, and the players grumbling about a lack of tactical vision and his team selection. When Wenger arrived they expected more of the same. 'No one trusted Wenger at first,' said Tetsuo Nakanishi, then a defender at Grampus. 'They all said, "Here comes another foreigner".'

The players' suspicions seemed justified by the lousy start to the season, which had put Wenger in a seemingly perpetual state of fury. When a player had the ball in training and looked to him for guidance on what to do next, Wenger just shouted back: 'Decide for yourself! Why don't you think it out?' Known in Europe for his cerebral approach to football, in Japan he appeared to be angry after every training session, and players didn't dare go near him the day after another loss. According to one report, when striker Takafumi Ogura missed a clear scoring chance, Wenger was heard yelling at him in English from the bench, 'I'll kill you!'

After a few months, however, Wenger began to win the team over. Stojkovic had played for Olympique Marseilles before Grampus, and told the other players about Wenger's reputation at Monaco. Wenger also began to give them a few of the detailed instructions they craved, like always to pass forwards when at all possible; and if not possible, then pass to the side; only pass back when forced to.

But Wenger's basic stance remained the same. Because a football game is in constant flux, players have to take the initiative and make decisions, not the manager. He showed them AC Milan videos – not because he wanted them to copy AC Milan, but so they could see how great players in a great team always worked to contribute, and force the opposition into the ideal position for them. 'I did not tell them, "When you're in this situation, pass to this player",' he explained. 'I knew it would take a long time to produce results, but there was no other way.'

The 1995 first stage took a break from mid-May to the end of June to make way for international matches. Going into this, Grampus had climbed off the bottom, but were still twelfth out of fourteen teams, having won six matches and lost ten. Wenger took them to Versailles for a ten-day camp, where they repeated basic training: skills, positioning and physical work. On their return Grampus hit a streak of form. The players began to understand how to play within tactical systems, as well as the key point that the player with the ball decides the next move. They became tougher mentally, and developed a new confidence. They were physically stronger, and conceded fewer second-half goals. Of the remaining ten games in the first stage, Grampus lost just one, and were unbeaten at home. They finished in fourth place, by far their highest position yet. They did even better in the second stage, coming in second. And in the post-season they won the Emperor's Cup, their first ever trophy.

Wenger's achievements at Grampus and the intelligent approach to football he represented gave him huge kudos in Japan. After joining Arsenal in 1996 and winning the double there in 1997/98, he became a perennial favourite for the position of Japan national team manager. Japanese players, too, remembered his coaching as something special. Defender Nakanishi wrote notes at home for thirty or forty minutes each day after training – not to revise before matches, but because 'I began to feel he was a great coach, and I thought they might be valuable.'

Wenger himself always talked about Japan with fondness, and once said the Japanese had given him back a love for the game. 'More than the wins,' he wrote of his time in Nagoya, 'I was proud of the quality of the soccer we were playing. This was a fantastic moment, when I suddenly saw a ray of light. I could touch the beauty of soccer as a team sport – the essential thing of it being full of individual expression at the same time as a team sport.'

CHAPTER SEVEN

Competition

Tests of skill and endurance have long been a regular feature of Japanese television, and the airwaves offer numerous eating contests to see who can eat the most sushi, dumplings or noodles in a given time; insomnia contests, where participants try to stay awake for two days while enduring sleep-inducing situations like warm, comfortable beds; and blind-tasting competitions to test contestants' ability to name the type of cake they are eating and the shop that made it. So as the Japanese came to like football, many also came to feel there were more interesting approaches to the game than just matches. When an early evening TV show called *Muscle Ranking* featured a football competition between two high schools, nothing as mundane as making them play a match against each other would compete adequately for the primetime audience. Instead, players from the two schools tried to hit targets with spot kicks. They carried on knocking boards out of frames till a player on one team failed, and so the other school won.

Most of the new football programmes on Japanese TV followed the same formula. To provide viewers with that little bit of added interest beyond match analysis and highlights, *Soccer 12* got J.League squads to take part in a juggling contest. They each tried to break a record set by a Cuban player who could run 100 metres in seventeen seconds while keeping the ball up. Another, *Super Soccer*, featured a power-shooting contest, in which players fired balls at a mini-goal as hard as possible and the velocity of their kicks was measured. Later it introduced a banana kick contest using two giant inflatable bananas. These stood vertically near the edge of the penalty area in line with the goalposts. From a few metres further back, players had to curl dead balls round these, shooting from positions that required as much bend as possible.

The Japanese loved skills and the art of perfecting movements. Schoolchildren started early, learning to write thousands of kanji ideograms by training their hands in the movements needed to execute each pen stroke in the correct order. Later, the way to learn anything – from cutting up sushi to learning a new dance step – was to study the proper motions and then repeat these again and again to draw gradually nearer perfection. Schools often taught football much as if it was tennis, and made boys repeat shots and crosses until their bodies learnt the movement perfectly – no matter that practising free of interference is completely different from battling shoulder-to-shoulder with a defender. In Japan's cramped, grassless city parks, instead of playing kick-around games, children mostly worked on their skills, often alone with a ball, juggling hundreds of times with different parts of their body. Even when they played in small groups, they simply practised passing to each other. 'The Japanese would prefer football to be scored like gymnastics instead of on goals,' said writer Kenji Ohba. 'If it was, "Great through-pass – 5.8", "Perfect trap – 6", then maybe we could beat the world.'

Maybe they could – and better still, they would then win while avoiding the one thing the Japanese found distasteful about sport: confrontation. For the Japanese, confrontation was the opposite of harmony, which they considered a defining quality of their culture in the way that Americans viewed freedom and Germans orderliness. In Japan group harmony implied consideration for others, and that members accept a hierarchy based on seniority. For players nurtured in high school sports clubs, these assumptions proved especially hard to kick.

Ignace Mofeka, a Congolese who played for Albirex Niigata when that team was in the Japan Football League, remembered a controversial session of four-versus-two – a warm-up game in which four players stand in a circle and pass the ball, while two inside try to intercept it; when one of the two steals the ball, he swaps places with the outside player who slipped up. In one such game, a younger player on the outside passed the ball to an older player, who mistrapped and gave it away. But the older player told the younger one to go inside, expecting him to obey as younger players usually did. On this occasion, however, the younger player refused to go inside, as he hadn't messed up. The older player suggested settling the issue using the paper-rock-scissors game. The younger player still refused though, and the older one hit him on the arm and insisted. 'This happened twice,' remembered Mofeka. 'Eventually the younger one gave in and they did *janken* – the rock, paper, scissors game – and the younger one went inside. Then when we started again, the older player again lost the ball and had to go inside. The younger player laughed and the older one was fuming.'

As well as order, harmony meant reluctance to blame teammates for mistakes. Ossie Ardiles, who managed several clubs in England before going to Japan, said this shyness made it hard to start constructive team discussions. 'In England the players like to participate,' he said. 'I put questions to them, like, "Why are we losing 2–0?" and got them to respond. Here it is impossible. They do believe in harmony. They will never complain about a teammate and say, "Why are you not doing this or that?" I have never seen Japanese fighting in the street, and I have never seen players fighting each other. I believe in harmony as well – but with more honesty.'

Harmony extended to relations between team coaches and the club management, and presented another test for the diplomatic skills of interpreters. During Ardiles's three years at Shimizu S-Pulse, Steve Perryman, who had played and later coached with him at Tottenham Hotspur, was his head coach. When Ardiles quit at the end of 1998 to go to Croatia Zagreb, the club asked Perryman to step up to manager. During negotiations over his contract, club managers told Perryman that he was inexperienced. In particular, they said, he had only been a coach rather than a full manager. Not true. Perryman had lots of experience, and he didn't appreciate this being overlooked. So he addressed the interpreter: 'Fucking tell them that I have had six jobs, including four as actual manager.'

The interpreter started translating into Japanese: '*Sumi-masen* . . .' – 'Please excuse me, but . . .'

This, Perryman thought, lacked his original nuance, and he asked the interpreter to rephrase: 'No,' he said. 'Fucking tell them like I said it.'

So the interpreter started again with, '*Sumimasen* . . .', but a bit louder than before.

Perryman loved coaching in Japan, and was full of praise for the work ethic of Japanese players. 'They're always coming at you for more [instruction],' he said, 'because they want to work, to improve. You have to take the ball off them and send them home after training.' As S-Pulse manager he led them to the second-stage championship in 1999, and after returning to England for a while, went back to coach then manage Kashiwa Reysol. Contract negotiations aside, he appreciated the good manners and cooperation that lubricated daily life in Japan. In competitive sport, however, the Japanese could reach inappropriate levels of gentility. Jorginho, a fiercely competitive member of Brazil's 1994 World Cup-winning side, played for Kashima Antlers for several years. In one game against S-Pulse, he scythed an opposition player to the ground. Seeing a teammate fouled like this, another S-Pulse player ran across the field towards the Brazilian. Jorginho glared and puffed himself up like a cockerel ready for a fight. 'Jorginho had cut our man in half, and I was thinking, "Go on!",' remembered Perryman. 'And our player shakes hands! I'm wondering, is he thinking, "Can I have your autograph – I always wanted to shake your hand"? We laughed like crazy on the bench.'

All technique and no friction could put a damper on football's competitive cut and thrust. In kick-around games, the Japanese normally didn't bother to keep score, preferring instead to do without the unpleasantness of one group claiming victory over another. Elegant passing build-ups and tricky dribbles received cheers and complements. Easy or messy goals were looked down on as vulgar. Lucky goals, like when a cross went in by mistake, drew embarrassed apologies from the scorer. Even in professional teams, foreign players noticed little of the rivalry they were used to – of wanting to win practice games and fight for their place in the team. Michael Pao, an American teammate of Ignace Mofeka's at Niigata, said: 'In practice games the day before a match, me and Iggy still hate losing. We are the only ones wanting to win. The others are just laughing. I'm not saying I want them to be stoic warriors. But they take it too lightly.'

So while foreign coaches taught the Japanese how to think more and worry less, probably the greatest contribution of the top foreign players who played in Japan was to convey the idea that winning really mattered. When Dragan 'Pixy' Stojkovic arrived in Japan, culture shock came not in the form of raw fish or bowing, but when he heard a team mate snoring. Stojkovic came to Nagoya Grampus in 1994 after his former team, 1993 European Cup winners Olympique Marseilles, unravelled following a match-fixing scandal. Soon after his arrival, Grampus played away to Gamba Osaka, and were leading 3–1 with 67 minutes elapsed. But they lost concentration, and by the end of the match had conceded another four goals to go down 5–3.

Stojkovic found it impossible to sleep after losing games, and regularly stayed up to five or six o'clock in the morning after defeats. After talking over every last detail of the game with his wife, he watched TV and played video games to kill the hours before tiredness got the better of his frustration. Getting on the team bus after his team had caved in so ignominiously, he prepared himself for an especially tortured version of this personal vigil, when he heard a sound from the seat behind him: one of his teammates had nonchalantly dozed off. 'I couldn't believe someone could forget about it as though it was just part of his daily work routine,' said Stojkovic later. Yukihiko Kimura, author of two books on Stojkovic, remembered: 'Pixy always complained, "Why do they laugh when they lose?"'

These frustrations, plus Grampus' slump under Gordon Milne, convinced Stojkovic he wouldn't last long in Japan. But Wenger's arrival persuaded him to stay on, and at a time when Yugoslavia was being torn apart by war Stojkovic found calm in Japan. 'Japan is a safe and rich country, and this is good for my family,' he said later. 'The people here are peaceful.'

Pixy's behaviour on the pitch was anything but peaceful. He quickly gained a reputation for a foul temper. He kicked over water bottles and field-side microphones, and cried as he left the field following a defeat in a semi-final of the Emperor's Cup. He had been sent off in his first game for arguing with the referee, and went on to pick up a total of thirteen red and seventy-two yellow cards in Japan – both records – including a streak of nine cautions in just ten games during the second stage of the 1999 season (he was suspended for the other games). When he knew the referee couldn't see, he greeted opposing fans with the gesture made by placing the left hand on the right upper arm, and punching upwards with the right fist.

In 1996, Stojkovic turned down an invitation from Wenger to join him at Arsenal. Eventually he stayed in Japan seven years, longer than any other top international footballer. He became the most revered foreign player in Japan, and the Grampus crowd adored him for his skill, vision and passion. In return he rewarded them with tricky back heels, volleys with the outside of his foot and mid-game juggling displays. But more than champagne football, he thought his main contribution to Japan came from the look on his face: 'I hate to lose a game,' he said, 'and this was difficult for me to explain to my teammates. So I talk to them via the interpreter before games. I tried to explain to them what is important for us to do on the pitch – that there is a big difference between losing and winning. But more than this, they understand from my face. My grimace is the most important thing.'

Another player who shattered the calm of Japanese football was Dunga, the fiery Brazilian midfielder. Not a naturally gifted player, he acknowledged that when he had been an apprentice with Internacional in his native Porto Alegre, plenty of other players had been more talented and skilful. But Dunga was stronger-willed than any of them, and his grit took him all the way to a career at Fiorentina and VfB Stuttgart, as well as the Brazilian national team. In the 1990 World Cup, he was part of a controversial defensive revolution that finally laid to rest the era of Brazilian flare and artistry. In 1994, he captained another defensive Brazil team, which won the World Cup on penalties after the only ever goalless final – probably the dullest in history, as Brazil and Italy both succeeded in playing for 120 minutes without making a single fatal mistake. It was a victory for defensive concentration. And how Dunga hated a lack of concentration.

He had first visited Japan in 1984, playing for Internacional in the Kirin Cup, an annual mini-tournament, and took the opportunity to absorb a little culture. He loved the elegance of Japanese ceramics and food, and admired the tea ceremony for its harmony, precision and lack of rough movement. So when he got the opportunity to play for Jubilo Iwata in 1995, one of the greatest motivations was the chance to become familiar with Japan's noble cultural traditions. He even owned some samurai armour whose headpiece he liked to try on from time to time. 'I thought the power of Japan was an essence that oozed from the inside of people,' he wrote later. 'I thought it was a power that, even if the individual was weak, could be generated by a group of people. In the past, the world competed to copy Japan's patriotism and samurai spirit. I thought that people would preserve this style of living ... But when I came to live in Japan, the images I had were smashed one after another, and each time I was shocked.'

The first jolt came in training. Younger players, apparently in awe of his reputation, didn't try to tackle him. And if he made a mistake, no one mentioned it, as if they were all trying to pretend nothing had happened. When the players did things wrong during real matches, they got flustered – visiting the touchline unnecessarily for nervous drinks of water, and anxiously speeding up their play when they should have been slowing down to regain their rhythm. Worst of all, they didn't care about their own mistakes in training, too often just repeating the same movements whether or not these produced results. If Dunga practised crossing and only six or seven out of ten went right, he was furious. And if he made the same mistake in a match having already been told about it during training, his anger 'reached a level where it cannot be controlled. But in this country, no one says anything even if you make a mistake.' It was all too much. 'I yearned for the high degree of learning and concentration of samurai I had learnt about in books,' he wrote at the time. 'But in the end, I now spend every day shouting "Concentrate!" at Japanese people.'

Dunga thought Japan's problem was that players treated football like just another day at work – and in a Japanese office at that, where results were nice, but deferment to the boss and maintaining a quiet life were more important. Asked by a magazine to compare Japanese and Brazilian football, he said: 'They're completely different. When Brazilian players are defeated in a match, they lose their appetite, withdraw inside themselves and get depressed. But when Japanese players lose, they're back to normal within five minutes. At the same time as being the greatest happiness, Brazilian football is a war when players clash with both extremes of emotion. For Japanese players, a match is a superficial thing and it doesn't matter whether they win or lose. Japanese football is like going to work at a company. It's a kind of job.'

And while the Japanese didn't understand how serious football was, neither did they know how to have proper fun.

The Japanese social occasions Dunga attended were full of stress, with everything carried out with military precision. At a barbecue, for example, everyone had to arrive punctually, and bringing along an uninvited guest was considered rude to the host. And everything had to be done properly, including the grill-master wearing white gloves. In short, unlike the samurai he admired, the modern Japanese seemed to do everything with the same middling degree of seriousness. 'The Japanese look the same whether they're working or playing. When we [Brazilians] have a party, we fool around putting ice down each others' shirts to have a good time, but Japanese find this disturbing. When the Japanese relax, they look like they're making an effort to relax.'

Another problem he identified in Japanese footballers was that they played like boy scouts. In Dunga's view, they lacked the element of cunning essential to Latin football that was known as *malícia* in Portuguese (and *malicia* in Spanish). These translate literally into English as 'malice', but in South America had more positive connotations of guile and craftiness – cheating or semi-cheating and getting away with it like, say, handling the ball into goal and pretending it was really a header. The Japanese were sorely lacking in *malícia*, not least because they all learned football at school, where the referee was usually a teacher. Even professionals, Dunga noted, stopped playing when the ball crossed the touchline, rather than carrying on till the referee blew his whistle. When they committed a foul, they sometimes raised their hands in apology, as if to turn themselves in.

Describing this black – or at least dark-grey – art in a book intended to educate the Japanese in hardboiled professionalism, he wrote: 'If my team is winning 2–0 near the end of a match, and I am fouled in a tackle, I pretend to be hurt badly, and lie on the ground not getting up. Even if the referee comes over, I say, "Sorry – wait a minute", and get up as slowly as possible. First I will pull my socks up and down several times. When I finish with my right leg, I will start on the left. I retie my boots, put the ball carefully in place, and then take a ten- or twenty-pace run-up for the free kick. But this free kick will just go to a player a metre away.'

Other techniques he suggested for a winning team included:

- In the opposition penalty area, first wait to be tackled, then release the ball at the last moment to get a penalty.
- Stand in front of your opponent when competing for a header, even when you have no chance of getting to the ball first. Then the opponent cannot move forward, and will not be able to head accurately.
- Again, even when you have no chance of heading the ball, jump shoulder-to-shoulder with an opponent, so he will lose his balance, and not be able to score. ('The reason Japanese players are weak at heading in front of the goal is that they only jump when it is possible for them to reach the ball.')

'These things are all within the rules,' he explained. 'I don't want to say they are very pure acts, but they mean you can win mentally over your opponent, like in a card game. You get him disturbed and irritated and put yourself in a superior position psychologically. These types of play are just intelligent. It means you are more intelligent and they are less intelligent. It is not cowardly or unfair.'

Malícia also included taking advantage of Japanese referees who were over-impressed by Dunga's World Cup-winning status and reluctant to show him a yellow card. After one decision he didn't like at Iwata, he turned to the home crowd with arms raised and thumbs pointed down, leading them in booing the referee. This is normally a booking offence, but Dunga got away without a caution.

These antics didn't work with everyone, though, and Dunga knew when to rein in this behaviour. To help raise the standard of Japanese refereeing – partly in response to the difficulties Japanese officials had with stronger-minded foreign players like Stojkovic and Dunga – the J.League employed Leslie Mottram, a FIFA referee who had officiated at Euro 1996. A Scot, and a schoolteacher to boot, Mottram was unimpressed by *malícia*. His first game in Japan was Marinos versus Jubilo – and he showed his first yellow card, after just twelve minutes, to Dunga.

'That is not a yellow card in Japan,' protested Dunga, trying to educate Mottram in the way referees should treat him.

Mottram was having none of it. 'I am Scottish,' he replied, 'and it is a yellow card.'

Unlike the temperamental Stojkovic, Dunga appeared to be firmly in control of his actions, and just hoping to gain advantage by pushing the limits of reasonable behaviour as far as possible. 'After that,' said Mottram, 'I never had to give him a yellow card again. He was a brilliant player, and it was a treat to be on the same field as him. Maybe Japanese referees were in awe of him . . . In Japanese culture it is very difficult to referee someone who has a high status like him.'

Under Dunga's influence, Jubilo became the sneakiest team in the J.League, constantly faking fouls and diving for penalties. They also became one of the most successful. Dunga's greatest contribution was to the players' attitude during matches. The first thing he did on arriving in Japan was to learn the Japanese for key words – 'Watch out!', 'Don't foul!', 'Cool down!', 'Wait!', 'Forward!', 'Right!' and 'Left!' – and from day one, he berated his teammates mercilessly. When he didn't know the Japanese, he shouted in Portuguese. His most common complaint was bad positioning: Japanese strikers tended to head for the far post, even though most crosses came to the near post. Another source of anger was crosses from deep in midfield that were too easy for opposition defenders to clear. And when he saw a striker attempting to dribble through a group of four defenders one minute, but then flinching from a one-on-one situation the next, he shouted: 'Can't you do sums!' He sometimes announced that if they had no will to play, he would go back to Brazil. But even after

Dunga left Jubilo, he remained an adviser, and his lessons stuck. By mid-2001 Jubilo had won four J.League stage championships, and become overall annual champions twice. They also won the Asian Club Championship, and their squad boasted some of Japan's top players, such as midfielder Hiroshi Nanami and striker Masashi Nakayama.

Dunga fascinated the Japanese for the spectacle he presented on the pitch. When he was worked up, the sinews on his neck looked fit to burst out of his skin as he lectured a teammate in front of thousands of fans, jabbing his index finger at his temple to demand more thought and concentration. Some players just took their humiliation. After midfielder Akira Konno let a Yokohama Flügels player dribble round him at the sideline, Dunga grabbed him first by the hair, and then by both shoulders and planted him in the place he should have been standing. The astonished Konno let his body go limp as Dunga manhandled him into position. Others fought back like angry children. Taking a similar mauling, defender Takahiro Yamanishi pushed Dunga, turned away from him, and even grabbed his shorts in an attempt to avoid a grilling. Striker Naohiro Takahara displeased Dunga one day with some fancy play that went wrong. He just walked slowly away with his head bowed as Dunga followed alongside, shouting as he pushed up the tip of his nose to show what he thought of Takahara's attitude. Just in case he had not made himself clear, Dunga told TV reporters after the game, 'Takahara is not a player in the class of Pele or Maradonna.'

These tirades were not limited to his career in Japan. When Brazil played Morocco in the 1998 World Cup, he laid into both Bebeto and Ronaldo for not following the team rules. But Dunga appeared to strike a special chord in Japan. Television showed selections of his greatest roastings, and viewers were fascinated by the spectacle of the big dog in the yard putting the young pups in their place. One such TV show first played the angry scenes for laughs, and then switched to syrupy music as the voiceover explained that this was Dunga's 'football classroom full of love', where he was the '*sensei* of the football field'.

One explanation was that Dunga reminded the Japanese of the tough love dolled out by their high school sports coaches. But a nickname the media gave Dunga suggested the fascination had deeper roots. According to an old Japanese, the most frightening things in life were thunder, fire and father. Intimidating fathers had mostly disappeared in modern Japan, replaced – at least in the popular imagination – by the downtrodden, overworked *salaryman* (company employee) father, who was scared of his boss and didn't have the time or self-confidence to teach his kids right and wrong. The image of Dunga demanding higher standards from youngsters brought back folk memories of stormy fathers, so that's what they called him: *Kaminari Oyaji*, or Daddy Thunder.

CHAPTER EIGHT

The Black Goalposts

When the Japanese beat South Korea in Doha in 1993, they had thought they were on the way to two World Cups.

Under João Havelange, its president from 1974 to 1998, FIFA had tried to spread football to all corners of the globe. It was especially keen on rich new markets, which is why the 1994 World Cup went to the United States. In exchange, it agreed to try again to set up a professional league. So when Havelange said in 1986 that he would like to hold the 2002 competition somewhere in Asia, Japanese football officials saw their chance. The Japanese economy was more than twice the size of the rest of Asia combined. Japan had already hosted a summer (Tokyo 1964) and a winter (Sapporo 1972) Olympic games, as well as the 1979 world youth football championship. All these made the bid plausible. And the early success of the J.League – and especially the vast amounts of money football generated in Japan – made the bid look positively attractive. South Korea had also formally notified FIFA that it would also like to host the World Cup. But this looked at first to be little more than a token challenge, and as Japan progressed through the qualifiers for USA '94, it appeared a shoo-in to host the 2002 tournament. Tadao Murata, the deputy chairman of the JFA, was quoted as saying during the final round of qualifiers in Doha: 'If Japan qualifies and South Korea fails, then Japan will be 99 per cent certain of winning its bid.'

And then, in the space of a few seconds on 28 October, Japan's football dreams collapsed. After Japan drew with Iraq and South Korea beat the North to qualify for USA '94, Korean Football Association (KFA) chairman Chung Mong-joon leapt into action. 'We will make an effort to be able to host the 2002 World Cup,' he now told a press conference. 'We have qualified for the World Cup finals three times in a row, and four times in total. Though Japan has never managed this once, we have succeeded four times.'

That was not all. Just in case any neutral reporters were not sure which way to direct their sympathies, press material distributed by the Korean bidding team contained reminders of the two nations' past history. Japan had annexed the Korean peninsula in 1910, and ruled it until the end of World War Two. During this time, the colonial government made Japanese the primary language in Korean schools and eventually made all Koreans take Japanese names. It also ran the economy in such a way that around a million impoverished Koreans left their country to work in Japan and Manchuria. This was followed during Japan's 1937–45 war with China and, from 1941–45, with the Allied powers, by the transportation of 1.2 million Koreans to Japan as forced labourers. Korea, the material went on to declare, had possessed just one great vehicle of protest against Japanese rule: football. As the Korean Football Association's website later described it: 'Football provided the only channel for the Korean people to release the wrath and hardships under the Japanese colonialism and one of the few means to keep alive the hopes for national independence.'

Like Japan, Korea's first contact with football came through the British navy. But while football in Japan started in a military academy and spread slowly through educational institutions, Korea's first contact with football was a kick-around. In 1882, the British warship *Flying Fish* was docked in Incheon, west of Seoul, when the crew decided they were sick of staying aboard. So they came ashore illegally and started playing football. On seeing some military police-men, they ran back on board, leaving the ball behind in their haste. It is said that the first Korean game of football was played when a group of children, who had been watching the sailors, found the ball and started kicking it around themselves.

Football soon became far more popular in Korea than Japan. While the sword-loving Japanese began to swing baseball bats, Koreans preferred football, perhaps because they were poorer and the game required less equipment. Teams from Kyungsung – the old name for Seoul – and Pyongyang played regular matches, and Korean teams even travelled to China to play against British military teams in cities like Shanghai. More importantly, football spread quickly via schools and local sports festivals.

The Japanese authorities banned political meetings after the 1910 annexation, and sports festivals became rare opportunities for speeches and rallies for independence. Football thus became linked to the nationalist movement, and the colonial government saw the game as a threat. According to a KFA official history, Korea's first football goal was built in 1914, at Paichai High School in Seoul. The founder, an American missionary, and two leaders of the nationalist movement decided that football was a good way for students to develop mental and physical strength that might help them in their struggle for independence. So they built goalposts in the school grounds: pine logs formed the posts, while two pieces of wood rested on top as a crossbar. The only problem was the colour, white, which was the national colour of Korea.

Through their ignorance of football, the Japanese police acquired the notion that the goalposts had been painted white not because that was the colour all goalposts were, but as a nationalist symbol. They came to the school, stopped a football match in mid-game, and ordered that the posts be taken down; otherwise, they would ban football altogether. So the school came up with the obvious solution. They painted the goalposts black.

Not only were they more enthusiastic, the Koreans soon became better at football than the Japanese. In 1926, a Korean select eleven toured Japan for the first time, and played eight matches against Japanese universities, winning five and drawing three. In 1935, Koreans started competing in the Japanese FA Cup, and a Seoul team thrashed Tokyo Bunri University 6–1 in the final. When Japan played in the Berlin Olympics the next year, beating Sweden 3–2 before succumbing 8–0 to Italy in the quarterfinals, the team contained a Korean player, Kim Yon-sik. Koreans protested that there should have been more of their players given their ability, and in the next few years the Japan national team that played in an East Asian championship contained up to four Koreans. Korea became independent in 1945, and in 1948 Kim Yon-sik went on to play in the Olympics again, this time for his own country.

A single East Asian berth was available for the 1954 World Cup in Switzerland, and only Japan and South Korea applied for it. Normally this would be simple. The countries would play two matches, one each at home, and the aggregate winner would go to Switzerland. But Japan and South Korea had still not normalised relations, and the nationalist President Syngman Rhee, known as the father of modern Korea, was against the idea of any sporting contact with the former colonial masters. However, Vice-President Lee Ki-boong, who was also president of the Korea Sports Council, thought a World Cup place would honour the country's new independence and celebrate its recovery from the war fought from 1950 to 1953 between the western-backed South and the communist North. So he tried the only way he knew to persuade the hard-line president: he appealed to his hatred of Japan.

Japan had modernised faster than Korea and the rest of Asia, and despite its defeat in World War Two, was still the big, sophisticated neighbour. For Koreans, thirty-six years of colonial rule had magnified their resentment and feelings of inferiority. However, Vice-President Lee told his boss Rhee there was one field in which Korea could beat Japan: football. 'Even from before we were liberated, we were always better than the Japanese at football,' he said, according to a documentary drama reconstruction shown later on South Korean television. 'It is a good opportunity to triumph over Japan . . . Whatever happens in other areas, we can certainly beat Japan at football.'

Persuaded, President Rhee agreed to the 1954 World Cup qualifiers – but on two conditions. First, both games must be held in Japan, because he refused to let any Japanese on Korean soil. Second, 'you can go,' he told head coach Lee Yu-hyon, 'but you must take responsibility. If you lose, you can throw yourselves into the Korea Straits,' the sea channel between Korea and southern Japan.

The two matches were set for March 1954, and three days before the first, Tokyo was blanketed by unusually hard snowfall. It was still snowing lightly on 7 March, the morning of the game. After most of the snow had been cleared from the pitch, petrol was used to melt the rest, leaving a muddy, cratered field, still frozen in patches, and with no more than a few blades of grass dotted around. The conditions were so bad that Korean head coach Lee suggested to his Japanese counterpart Shigemaru Kakenokoshi that they postpone the game. Kakenokoshi, possibly sensing some weakness in the Koreans, insisted that they go ahead.

It was a terrible decision. The Korean winter is far colder than Japan's, with temperatures staying below minus ten centigrade for days on end, and the Korean players were used to harsh conditions. They were also motivated. First, they were keen to avoid death by drowning. And, despite playing away, the crowd of around 8,000 in Tokyo was over half Korean – mostly Koreans who had settled in Japan after going to work there during the colonial period. Moreover, most of the Korean players had grown up under colonial rule and been forced to receive their education in Japanese. For them, the match was the first time they had seen their national flag raised alongside that of their former master, providing a visual confirmation of their new independence.

The Koreans played simple kick–and-rush tactics, and booted long balls upfield and over the mud for their hard-running forwards to chase. The Japanese tried to build attacks slowly through a short passing game, and got bogged down in the mire. The Koreans were physically strong – naturally bigger than the Japanese, and toughened up by running during their cold winter; many appeared to be sweating during the match, with steam rising from their bodies. The Japanese were used to milder conditions – and were wearing short-sleeved shirts, not having any others. By halftime South Korea were 2–1 ahead, and the frozen Japanese players asked for buckets of hot water to thaw their feet. Some were so cold they couldn't wait to take their boots off, and they put their feet in the buckets with their boots still on, meaning they got colder still in the second half. Korea scored three more goals in the second half, and walked away with the match 5–1. Japan's right half Koji Miyata said afterwards: 'I had no feeling below my knees.' Another Japanese player, Osamu Yamaji, said: 'I felt sleepy during the game. They say that when you freeze to death you feel sleepy. It was like that. I couldn't think. So we couldn't stop them. My body just wouldn't move.'

A week later, in sunny weather, the two sides drew 2–2. South Korea went to Switzerland.

Koreans never stopped caring that they could beat Japan at football. Following Rhee's loss of power in 1960, Japanese athletes were allowed into Korea, and the nations played regular matches in most years from then on. But South Korea did not yield a victory to the Dettmar Cramer-trained Japan teams of the 1960s, and in thirty-one matches in the 1970s and 1980s only allowed the Japanese four victories. So when they lost to Japan in Doha, Koreans were horrified and the *Seoul Sports* newspaper ran the headline 'Disgrace'.

Behind this lingering resentment lay an inability by Japan and Korea to put the past behind them. Japan and the South normalised relations in 1965, but Japan never made amends as the Koreans wanted. Japan paid financial reparations, but not enough, many Koreans thought. Japanese emperors expressed regrets for colonial rule. But for Koreans these came years too late, and in terms that were too guarded – specifically, avoiding an actual apology: Emperor Showa (Hirohito) talked of his 'sincere regret' for the 'unfortunate past' when the South Korean president visited in 1984, while his successor Akihito upgraded these expressions to 'deep regret' over the 'suffering' of the Korean people under Japanese rule. In revenge, Seoul banned the import of Japanese culture, including films, comics and magazines.

Every time relations appeared to be improving, a new problem arose to provoke more trouble, usually when a Japanese politician put his foot in his mouth, like in 1986, when education minister Fujio Masayuki declared that Korea was partly responsible for its 1910 annexation, and in 1995, when former foreign minister Michio Watanabe claimed that 'both sides have now recognized the legitimacy of the annexation treaty'. Even when these politicians kept quiet, school history textbooks provided a constant source of friction, as Seoul and Beijing formally objected to versions authorised by the Japanese government that they thought whitewashed Japanese brutality. Relations took another dive in the early 1990s, when it was revealed that Japan's imperial army had organised 'comfort women' – mainly Korean and Chinese women forced to provide sexual services – for its soldiers during World War Two.

After each flare-up, Koreans were hurt and angry. Some Korean restaurateurs refused entry to visiting Japanese, crowds burned Japanese flags outside Tokyo's embassy in Seoul and even burned an effigy of then-prime minister Ryutaro Hashimoto during a 1996 dispute over the sovereignty of an uninhabited island called Takeshima in Japanese or Tokto in Korean. In response, the Japanese whispered amongst themselves about how 'emotional' their neighbours were, and pretended there was no problem.

The bidding for the 2002 World Cup provided another opportunity to play out this drama. The Japanese appeared almost nonchalant. Japan's bidding committee offered to set up a fund to promote football internationally, and otherwise relied on its reputation as a rich, highly organised country. Aside from a proposal for 'virtual stadia', to project live images of games for fans unable to get tickets for the later stages of competition, the main thrust of its argument was Japan's infrastructure. A brochure boasted of a motorway network scheduled to expand to 10,000 kilometres by the turn of the century, 270-kilometre-per-hour bullet trains linking the proposed match venues, and nearly half a million hotel rooms nationwide. In fact, the most visible activity in Japan was from Japanese fans. In November 1995, a FIFA delegation was scheduled to watch Kashima Antlers play Cerezo Osaka at the National Stadium. Though plenty of Antlers fans would make the two-hour bus ride to Tokyo, few Cerezo supporters were going to pay for the three-hour bullet train ride from Osaka. So supporters' groups from other J.League teams came along to make up a noisy, colourful crowd of 47,000. In preparation for a helicopter flyover of Kashima, which was hoping to host World Cup matches, an Antlers supporter called public offices and schools and got them to organise kids to play football in every part of the town while the delegation flew over.

Japan's hardcore fans aside, the Koreans were far more enthusiastic. World Cup theme festivals were held across the country, radio stations saturated the airwaves with 'We Are One', a World Cup song by pop group Koreana, and all three TV networks ran daily football specials. The bidding committee laid on a motorcade at Seoul airport for a visiting FIFA inspection team and entertained them lavishly. South Korea also pledged to donate all profits from the finals to the advancement of football. Most important was the tireless campaigning of KFA chairman Chung. In 1994, Chung had beaten JFA deputy chairman Murata in an election to produce an Asian vice-chairman of FIFA. Chung was the son of Chung Ju-yung, the founder of the Hyundai industrial group. As well as a FIFA vice-president, he was the chairman of Hyundai Heavy Industries and a member of parliament. He had an MBA and a Ph.D. from American universities and spoke English fluently and gave good speeches, and soon Korea had secured the support of UEFA chairman Lennart Johansson, who was the most influential FIFA vice-president and brought with him the votes of most other Europeans and Africans on the FIFA executive committee.

And, inevitably, Korea marshalled its historical pain. KFA chairman Chung said at one point that, 'it would be unfortunate for the people of Asia if [Japan] controlled everything in Asia with its economic power. That is felt especially by countries where, in the not so distant past, Japan recorded some sad history.' Japan tried to stay aloof from this fray, and JFA chairman Ken Naganuma said: 'I don't want to argue against this. I don't want to talk about that kind of old thing ... Japan will not interfere with South Korea at all. We will go our own way.' The head of the Korean bidding committee, Koo Pyung-hui, said: 'Our pride and history demand that we beat Japan. If we lose, it will hurt us greatly.' But when former Japanese prime minister Kiichi Miyazawa was asked about 'the painful special relationship between Japan and Korea', he replied: 'I don't think there is such a thing.'

Warming up for a Dynasty Cup match between the countries in Hong Kong in February 1995, Korean players started kicking balls against a wall in front of the Japan supporters. The reason was an advertising board at the base of the wall, paid for by a Japanese company and reading: '2002 WORLD CUP JAPAN'. When the Japanese fans realised what was going on they were angry and started shouting abuse, after which the Korean player kicked balls at them in the stands. Eventually a Japanese fan who went down on the pitch to protest got into a scuffle with a Korean player.

Amid this strife, politicians and FIFA officials saw an opportunity to use football to do what the two countries had failed at for the past half century: to cooperate on something. In spring 1994, Havelange was quoted as saying he would consider seriously the idea that Japan and South

Korea jointly host the 2002 World Cup. Later that year, Japanese foreign minister Yohei Kono told his Korean counterpart Han Seung-joo that he 'would like to avoid a situation where one side is left with bad feelings'. Given the circumlocution customarily employed by Japanese politicians, this amounted to a government endorsement of joint hosting. Japan's influential *Asahi* newspaper, too, began to run approving editorials, one saying, 'It would be good to aim for joint hosting,' and another asking, 'Could this be the kick-off for friendship?' In July 1995, Korean prime minister Lee Hong-koo told parliament: 'I would like the World Cup bidding to benefit Korea–Japan relations, and deal with it in a way that does not cause a split.' Press materials distributed after this speech added: 'The prime minister's comment indicated a favourable view towards joint hosting by Japan and Korea.'

The great thing about joint hosting was that no one lost. South Korea was rewarded for its long reign at the top of Asian football. Japan was rewarded for its recent uptake of the game and the sponsorship money it would generate. On 31 May 1996, FIFA awarded the 2002 World Cup to Japan and South Korea, the first time ever the competition would be hosted jointly by two nations.

Five months later, on 6 November, a FIFA committee decided that both host countries could participate without having to qualify, and Japan achieved a place in the World Cup finals for the first time ever.

CHAPTER NINE

Welcome To Blue Heaven

For most countries, playing in a World Cup for the first time is a joy and source of national pride. For Japan, if it achieved entry on the basis of its facilities and the money it could generate, 2002 would be an embarrassment – a confirmation of every bubble-era cliché about the Japanese buying up whatever they wanted in the world. To prestige buildings in New York and the trophy Van Goghs and Monets that adorned the headquarters of large Japanese corporations would now be added participation in the world's greatest sporting festival – not earned on the pitch, but bought. Indeed, Kazu Miura had just played for a year at Genoa, who were then in Italy's Serie A, in a deal that appeared driven by Japanese money as well as Kazu's ability: at the same time that Kazu signed, Kenwood, a maker of in-car hi-fi equipment, agreed to sponsor the club. Kazu only lasted a year in Genoa, and played in just twenty-one games, many as a substitute. He was later moved to deny that he had only played in the Serie A because of Kenwood's backing. 'It's easy for people to say I played because I had a sponsor,' he told an interviewer. 'But it was me who played out on that ground.' In the World Cup there was just one way Japanese football could redeem itself, and look forward to 2002 with pride: qualify for France in 1998.

To stand a chance, Japan needed to finish in the top two of a group including South Korea, the United Arab Emirates, Uzbekistan and Kazakhstan. The first of these matches pitted Japan against Uzbekistan in Tokyo, and the National Stadium was a beautiful sight. Built for the 1964 Olympics, it was a graceful elliptical structure, low on the 'main stand' side with its VIP seats and broadcast booths, and curving upwards at the 'back stand' opposite. Under an ink-black sky, red and white national flags waved against the background of a packed crowd dressed in blue, Japan's team colour. The Olympic torch burned bright orange above a blue and white board saying: 'Road To France'.

By the mid-1990s the national team was beginning to take on a new importance for Japan. In 1992, a group of fans calling themselves the Nippon Ultras, after the 'ultra' gangs at Italian clubs, had begun following the team to all its games at home or overseas. Led by Asahi Ueda, a genial young man with shaggy, dyed-brown hair, the Ultras believed strongly that they were there to do a job – to help the team win – and Japan games rarely featured any of the booing that other national teams had to put up with. Megaphone in hand, Ueda gave cues in a voice worn to a sandpapery rasp from a life of beer and shouting, and other fans returned his calls of 'Ni-ppon!' or joined in the Reds-created 'Warrior' chant.

The Ultras had started off as a small band of fanatics, but by 1997 the movement had spread. As supporters behind both goals warmed up for the Uzbekistan game with some pre-kick-off chants, Ueda noticed that people in the main stand were also chanting along. In the back stand opposite this, flags were shaking in time. Behind the goal, Ueda waved his megaphone and quietened down the supporters around him. Then he turned round towards the pitch and said: 'Hello, everyone in the main stand! It's time for the final qualifying rounds that everyone's been waiting for.' Old people in the expensive seats stood up and cheered in reply. 'If you like,' invited Ueda, 'why not chant "Nippon" with us? ... NI-PPON!'

The drummer pounded out three beats, and the older fans joined in, shouting 'Ni-ppon! (da, da, da), Ni-ppon! ...'

'Thank you for your cooperation,' said Ueda. 'Please support with us not just now, but throughout the game. Now, where shall we go? Next ... the back stand.'

Soon the whole stadium shook in time. One of the Ultras

had distributed twenty large cardboard boxes filled with scraps of paper throughout the crowd to make an Argentine-style confetti shower. When the game kicked off, thousands of supporters threw handfuls of paper in the air, where it hung in the sky, flickering in the stadium lights.

Before kick-off, strikers Kazu Miura and Shoji Jo knelt together in the centre circle with their hands on the ball and said a few words of prayer. Then Japan ripped the Uzbek defence apart with clever through passes, and finished the first half 4–0 in the lead. In the second half they became casual, and conceded three goals while scoring two more. Still, the 6–3 victory provided just the kind of thrills these new supporters had come for.

Among the observations made by foreign players and coaches about Japanese football was that teams went through striking mood swings. When they were winning, they played well, but they then sometimes began to think it was all too easy. And when their backs were against the wall, heads went down, and the team took on an air of dejection. The qualifying campaign for the 1998 World Cup started on just such a roller-coaster ride.

The inconsistency displayed in the Uzbekistan game set the pattern to come, and Japan somehow contrived to throw matches away. At home to old rivals South Korea, Japan went ahead after twenty-two minutes of the second half, but then collapsed at the end, conceding an equaliser in the thirty-ninth minute followed by the Korean winner just three minutes later. Away to Kazakhstan, they were 1–0 up after twenty-two minutes and dominated the rest of the game – but again conceded points at the end, letting in an equaliser with just one minute left on the clock. Against the UAE in Tokyo, Japan had a dream start when recently naturalized Brazilian Wagner Lopes fired an impossible-looking long-range goal from the right-hand edge of the penalty area. But they soon lost their rhythm, conceded an equaliser with ten minutes left of the first half, and failed to score in the second. With just two matches left, South Korea and the UAE held the top two positions in the group, and Japan could no longer be certain of qualifying even if they won their remaining games. When the final whistle blew this time, the crowd's normally sunny mood disappeared. Some fans booed, and then the ground went quiet. Scuffles broke out between supporters in some parts of the stands. As the players left the stadium to board the team bus, dozens of fans who didn't share Asahi Ueda's ideas on positive support surrounded the area and showered the team with abuse. Some climbed onto television broadcast vans. Others pelted the bus with plastic bottles, cans and eggs, and shouted, 'Bring out Kazu!' because Japan's best player had failed to score since his opening game hat trick.

This outburst of public frustration marked a turning point. By this time, manager Shu Kamo had been fired and replaced by his number two, Takeshi Okada. Just forty-three years old, Okada was a modern coach who had spent time as a player training with West Ham, and later studied coaching in Germany. With Okada in charge and the public demanding results, the team slowly began to play with a new sense of purpose. As group winners, South Korea had already qualified, and they sat back for their game with Japan in Seoul. Japan won 2–0, only their second victory ever in Seoul, and the UAE drew with Uzbekistan. Japan were back on track, and the last game, against Kazakhstan in Tokyo, was played in a party mood. The Ultras distributed 20,000 rolls of paper tape – 10,000 blue and 10,000 white – which fans threw into the sky as the players took the field, so they glistened under the floodlights. Kazu was suspended for a second yellow card against South Korea, and Masashi Nakayama returned to the team in his place. Celebrating a goal he scored at the end of the second half, he pulled up his shirt to reveal another shirt underneath – Kazu's number 11, which he had been wearing because Kazu couldn't bear to be away from the occasion. Japan won 5–1, putting them in second place in the group, and securing a play-off against Iran to go to France. Before the match had begun, the Ultras floated a vast blue and white banner over one of the stands, which summed up the mood. It contained a smiley face and the words: 'Welcome to Blue Heaven.'

The traditional career path for a Japanese footballer had started with four years of university, after which a player would join a large corporation with a football team. The generation that played for Ooft at Doha turned (officially) professional mid-career, when their corporate teams entered the J.League, or they quit one of the lesser corporate teams to join a J.League club. But the footballers that grew up with the J.League were different. They had turned professional straight after high school, at age eighteen, and most had been aiming to play world-class football from when they were kids.

Goalkeeper Yoshikatsu Kawaguchi, though attending school in provincial Shizuoka prefecture, was exposed to world football from the age of about fifteen. His school, Shimizu Shogyo (Vocational) High School, already invited Brazilian coaches for periods ranging from several months to over a year. And when Kawaguchi showed his talent, the head coach arranged for him to spend a month at Internacional in southern Brazil. The goalkeeper coach there, Edinho, rated Kawaguchi too. 'It was the first time a foreign coach had said that I was good,' said Kawaguchi. 'Being recognised – especially at that age – makes you really happy.' After that, Edinho came to Japan so he could coach at Kawaguchi's school full-time.

In addition, Kawaguchi learned a new attitude to football at Internacional, where he spent his month in a dormitory with Brazilian apprentices his own age. 'They were aiming to be professionals so they could help their families,' he remembered. 'They trained very hard, and never slacked off. And in the top team training sessions the standard was really high, and lots of fans turned up to watch. I decided I wanted to play somewhere like this in the future.' Even back in Japan, Kawaguchi was exposed to players from other countries in a competition called the SBS Cup, an international youth tournament organised by a Shizuoka TV station. Participants over the years included the youth teams of clubs like Vasco da Gama, Real Madrid and Ajax, and players such as Nicolas Anelka, Patrick Kluivert (later of Ajax, Barcelona and Holland) and Cafu (Roma and Brazil). Said Kawaguchi of his generation: 'From this age, we were always thinking about foreign soccer and the outside world.'

When players of this age turned professional, they tasted even more world football. Even if they weren't being lectured by Dunga on their responsibilities, or taught to be more creative by Arsène Wenger, they were playing on a weekly basis against the likes of Stojkovic and Brazilian international Leonardo.

On the back of this, Japan's under-23 team qualified for the Atlanta Olympic Games in 1996, the first time Japan had reached the Olympics since 1968. Sportswriter Tatsuhito Kaneko labelled them 'Generation A'. The A was partly for Atlanta, but also because they were simply used to playing alongside or against A-class footballers. Their predecessors in the Japan national team had thought it a great achievement to beat South Korea. But even though the first match in Atlanta was against mighty Brazil, Generation A were unfazed. Waiting for the kick-off, Kaneko reported, midfielder Ryuji Michiki told himself simply that Ze Maria, the right back he would face, was not as good a player as Jorginho, the former Brazilian international who played for Kashima Antlers. Michiki had played against Jorginho in the J.League, so figured he didn't have too much to worry about. Defender Naoki Matsuda said that at the same moment, he 'couldn't stop laughing . . . The moment I thought I was about to play Brazil in a real match with fans round the world watching, for no particular reason, I just felt this surge of joy well up inside me.'

Not only were they relaxed, they won the match 1–0. They were a bit lucky: the winner was the result of a mix-up between Brazilian defender Adair and goalkeeper Nelson

Dida, and would have been an own-goal had midfielder Teruyoshi Ito not rushed forward to poke the ball home. But the result, against a team that contained Roberto Carlos, Bebeto and Rivaldo, also came from a level of skill, organisation and self-belief that had not previously existed in Japan. Kawaguchi, who kept goal in the Atlanta Olympics, said later: 'The Japanese used to have a kind of complex,' about world-class opposition. 'But after we beat some foreign teams, we gained confidence that we could win. It's experience.'

The national team aiming to qualify for France was a mixture of old and new. Left over from the Ooft era were players like Kazu Miura and defender Masami Ihara, the captain. New additions included Kawaguchi, striker Shoji Jo (his once-shaved hair now grown out to a wavy mop), and attacking midfielder Hidetoshi Nakata.

Nakata, instantly recognisable for hair that varied in colour between shades of tea, mustard and marmalade, was a player unlike any Japan had seen before. Mentally tough, he never lost his cool on the field, and shrugged off any mistakes he made. He was also brainy, with an IQ of 129, and played football as a kind of high-speed chess. More than goals, he regarded the highpoints of the game as defence-splitting passes.

Unlike every other football-mad Japanese child, he had not been interested in overseas football, and never watched *Diamond Soccer* on TV. He didn't even watch the World Cup, deciding that it was better to sleep properly than stay up into the small hours to see games broadcast from other time zones. 'Just because you really yearn to play like someone, that doesn't mean you can do the same,' he explained in a memoir. 'If you could become good by imitating how foreigners played, maybe I'd watch them, but that's not true.' For Nakata, football was about thinking it out for yourself. Nakata had an ideal in his head for the type of football he wanted to play. 'I like things like maths and physics where you use formulae and laws to end up with the only correct answer,' he said. 'It's easy to play football if you think about it mathematically ... I go after the ball according to a football "formula" ... There is always a theory in my head.'

This gap between the game in his head and reality on the pitch was his main source of both motivation and frustration, and had reduced him to tears on occasion. The object of practice, he said, was to acquire the skills needed to bridge the gap. When a new manager had been appointed at his club, Bellmare Hiratsuka, Nakata put in a special request for a training partner with whom he could simply practise passing. Then he would pass the ball back and forth, learning the effect of different amounts of pressure applied by different parts of the foot. 'I repeat passes until the type of pass and its speed become the same as the image I have. By practising this, you can eventually pass the ball without always having to look down at it.' The result was a distinctive posture. With or without the ball, he ran bolt upright, his head flicking from side to side, as if he was carrying out Terminator-style instant snapshots and analysis of the game around him. For Nakata, still just twenty, Japan's World Cup play-off on 16 November 1997 was his night to shine.

The play-off against Iran was set for the Larkin Stadium in Johor Bahru, a city at the southern tip of the Malay Peninsula, just north of Singapore. The losers would not quite be out of it: they would get a second shot at France by playing Australia, winners of the Oceania qualifying group. But the strain was telling on the Japan team. They had all spent over two months living in hotel rooms and making long trips to the Middle East and obscure parts of central Asia, and had even suffered booing and abuse from a minority of their own fans. Manager Okada said later that the squad was mentally and physically exhausted.

The efforts of Asahi Ueda and the other Ultras had paid off handsomely and they now led the support of a nation swept up by the drama of the campaign. About 15,000 Japanese travelled to Johor Bahru. Some took time off work; others quit their jobs when told they couldn't have a day off. The Ultras distributed paper tape and blue plastic bags to the Malaysians who made up the rest of the sell-out crowd of 20,000 and joined in chants of 'Ni-ppon!' Though Johor Bahru had been selected as a neutral venue, the atmosphere was that of a Japan home game.

In the thirty-ninth minute, Nakayama set the crowd alight. Nakata picked up the ball in the Iranian half a few yards in front of the centre circle. With his second touch he threaded a perfect through-ball between two Iranian white shirts putting Nakayama free. Onside, Nakayama collected Nakata's pass, and keeping his nerve slotted the ball away.

Japan went into the break 1–0 up, but after just one minute of the second half, Kawaguchi parried a shot from striker Ali Daei, who played in Germany for DSC Arminia Bielefeld and would later join Bayern Munich. Khodadad Azizi of FC Cologne pounced on the rebound and knocked in Iran's equaliser. Thirteen minutes later, Daei saw a cross coming in high from the right, out-jumped the Japanese defence, and scored Iran's second.

Two-one down, Okada took off Kazu and Nakayama, and brought on Jo and Lopes. Kazu said later he had just been checking because he couldn't see the signs by the side of the pitch clearly. But from his expression, it looked like he simply couldn't believe that he, Japan's finest player, was being substituted. He pointed at his chest and asked: 'Me?'

The substitution soon paid off though, and again the set-up came from Nakata. He crossed the ball from the left precisely onto the head of Jo around the penalty spot, who headed in the equaliser.

With the score tied 2–2 after ninety minutes, the game went into extra time, and Okada brought on Masayuki Okano, the fastest player in Japan, and speedier than most others in the world. When he was in full flight, his knees seemed to rise to chest level, and his long mane of black hair extended horizontally behind him. He had run 100 metres in 10.8 seconds and used to stage races against dogs

147

in order to get some competition. But he was not skilful, and had not played at all during the final qualifying rounds. When he didn't even make the bench for home games, he watched from the public stands, he told *Young Sunday* comic later. Once, standing at a urinal, he saw a fan wearing his number 14 shirt with 'Okano' written on the back. The fan didn't even notice him, and left the toilet without throwing him a glance.

Still, Okada figured Okano's lightning speed might cause problems for an exhausted Iranian defence. Okano immediately began to run them ragged – and send most of Japan into fits of despair and frustration. Just a minute into extra time, he tore away from the white shirts to put himself one-on-one with Iranian goalkeeper Ahmad-Reza Abedzadeh, but then fired straight at his chest. After 104 minutes, he was put free on a counterattack, and speeded ahead of Iranian defenders in helpless pursuit. But then, with time and space either to shoot or to dribble round Abedzadeh, he paused and instead passed left, across the goal to the advancing Nakata. But the hesitation had given two Iranians enough time to get between him and Nakata, and one of them cleared the ball. The normally expressionless Nakata threw his arms in the air in despair and disbelief. Okano got another chance just a minute later, when the ball rolled out beyond the goal area after a scramble in front of the Iranian goalmouth. Unchallenged, Okano hurtled in – and hoofed the ball high over the bar.

Early in the second period of extra time, Japan were lucky when Daei shot over the bar from close range, but after this the game was deadlocked. Then, two minutes from the end of extra time, Nakata picked the ball up a little forward of the centre circle. This time, he decided to go by himself. He dribbled a full circle to send an Iranian in the wrong direction, and then ran forward into space. Approaching the penalty area, he unleashed a hard left-foot drive between two defenders. Goalkeeper Abedzadeh dived to the ground and could only manage to push the shot away with the tips of his fingers. Okano was there again. This time, however, instead of a regular shooting stance, he fell on his side, collapsing his left leg, and sliding on it. He kicked the rebounding ball hard and low into the net.

The intensity of this last-minute drama sent Japan temporarily crazy over a game that had, until a few years previously, rarely blipped on the national radar. New football shows appeared on television, and the lives of national team members became a staple of daytime TV and gossip magazines. Nakata was anointed star of the moment, and everything from his fashion sense to his personality became subject to excessive scrutiny. He could no longer venture out in public without being mobbed, and his club's games suddenly attracted hundreds of girl fans. They shrieked when he got the ball. They greeted his spot kicks with camera flashes. As he came off the field after one game, one girl threw him several red roses.

Football also became a prism through which to discuss the nation's ills and how to mend them. Nakata in particular became a source of debate. Not only was he the youngest regular member of the national team, he was also the least deferential. A clip from the Iran match run repeatedly on television showed Nakata shouting at Ihara, who was the team captain, ten years his senior, and earning a record one hundred and tenth cap. More than just the shouting, what stood out was the manner in which Nakata addressed him: not the polite 'Ihara-*san*!' – but a simple 'Ihara!'

Nakata thought hierarchy on the football field was nonsense. 'When you're on the pitch,' he said, 'the players are equal, and there shouldn't be any hierarchy. When you are trying your very best to win, there is no time to think about what language you are using or what someone's attitude is like.' So at school he stood out – and made a few enemies – by not adding '-*san*' to the names of players in higher academic years than him. He also told younger boys that they should forget what year he was in during games, and just call him 'Nakata' without the '-*san*'. Though almost every J.League club wanted to sign him after high school, Nakata decided to join Hiratsuka Bellmare because, 'there are no hierarchical relations, and there was an environment where I thought I could be free.'

Ihara didn't mind Nakata's attitude: 'In fact it's Nakata who powers the team,' he said. 'He's the one who moves the players. When you're running after the ball, you don't think about who is older and who is younger. It's accepted that Nakata doesn't use "-san" when talking to other players.' But some older Japanese took Nakata's cool for disrespect, and even criticised him as a bad example to children. Turned overnight into Japan's new star, reporters and photographers tracked his every move. Nakata was naturally camera-shy and had been misquoted in newspapers in the past, and he hated the attention. So he refused to give interviews, told annoying photographers to get lost, and when he absolutely had to talk – like to a TV interviewer after a televised game – he sulked and gave the briefest, least informative replies he could. After he referred to a group of reporters as 'idiots', they made an official complaint to Bellmare.

Other Japanese saw the young star as a beacon of hope for the nation. Nakata was smart, independent, and free of the tired old ways that were holding Japan up. *President*, a magazine aimed at business executives, put him on its cover, and editor Hisayuki Kanda explained, 'Japanese organisations are trying to do away with their pyramid structure and flatten out. Nakata pays little regard to vertical relations and symbolises the new values of young people. He leads the team even though he's still young, and shows how this can work.' Nakata's friend the novelist Ryu Murakami, went even further, and called him 'a new symbol of modernised Japan'.

In contrast to Nakata's ascent, the 31-year-old Kazu's dip in form of the previous year turned into a full-scale slump. The shock substitution in Johor Bahru seemed to have marked the end of his years of peak form. His game became full of errors, and the goals dried up. The Iran game had been the first national team game for years in which he had either not been played or been taken off. Now, during the World Cup warm-up period, he appeared only in a few less important games. At a camp in Switzerland in May, when Okada finally picked the squad of twenty-two he planned to take to France, he left Kazu out.

Kazu got over the shock by going to Italy for a few days and peroxiding his hair. Other Japanese didn't cope so well. Commentators thought his being dropped reflected the changing values of Japanese society – away from traditional values like respect for seniority and lifetime employment at a single company, and towards globalisation. Chikushi Tetsuya, the respected presenter of the late-night television news magazine *News23*, pointed out that Kazu wasn't the only veteran to be cut from a World Cup side at the last minute – it had also happened in Brazil (Romario) and England (Gascoigne). The point, he explained, was that football followed global standards – a mantra in Japan at the time – and Japan was slowly starting to do the same. Despite a tradition in larger Japanese companies of never laying off full-time staff, economic hard times were forcing them to rethink, and dump older employees who had outlived their usefulness – a bit like Kazu. Chikushi asked his audience: 'Is this really the society we want to live in?'

For some people the answer was a clear no. Loyal Kazu fans flooded websites with protests and encouragement. Extremist Kazu fans posted death threats to manager Okada, or phoned him to say, 'We can't guarantee the safety of your family.' His house in Zushi, on the Pacific coast south of Yokohama, was put under a 24-hour police guard, and his children were taken to school by car instead of walking as they usually did.

The roots of this brief World Cup mania went deeper than a love of sport. Despairing of the lack of football in Japan in the 1980s, Ultras leader Asahi Ueda had persuaded his parents to send him to a Japanese school in England so he could play and watch the game more. Living there, he learned not only about football, but also about national identity. Sometimes, watching matches or out in the street, he was pointed at and called 'Jap', which the Japanese consider a racial slur. Playing football, he thought team-mates didn't pass to him because he was Japanese. In addition to such low-grade racism, he also noticed the easy patriotism the English seemed to enjoy. The Union Jack was ever-present in English football grounds, and whenever the opportunity arose they sang 'God Save the Queen' at the tops of their voices. 'Things like that made me decide to take more pride in being Japanese,' he told an interviewer later. 'I thought, why could they do this? Why can't we do this in Japan? Hardly anyone in Japan consciously thinks, "I'm Japanese".'

More than a feeling to unite the nation, patriotism in Japan had been a divisive problem. On the one hand, conservative politicians angered Asians by making light of Japanese wartime aggression and visiting Yasukuni Shrine, where Class A war criminals were honoured. A small minority of right-wingers staged occasional violent attacks on newspaper offices, carried out much more frequent intimidation against the media, and drove sound trucks round cities blasting propaganda, military songs and abuse through loudspeakers. At the same time, left-leaning Japanese worried about a return to the militarism of the war years, and thought even the moderate degree of patriotism found in most countries might put Japan on a slippery slope back to its disastrous past.

For the most part, national pride was not something the post-war Japanese expressed in the open. A few drinks might bring out feelings of resentment towards the West and superiority towards other Asians. But broadly speaking, most Japanese didn't feel that good about themselves as a nation. Defeat in World War Two had produced lingering feelings of national inadequacy, which were reinforced by a relationship with the United States that underlined Japan's dependence and inferiority. Japan officially had no military – the fighter jets, warships and tanks in its services were 'self-defence forces', forbidden by the constitution to fight overseas – and instead relied on the US for protection. More than their own culture, the Japanese increasingly took up that of the West.

To preserve some kind of identity against this onslaught, the post-war Japanese formed an idea of themselves as a 'unique' people – and not just unique in the way that every country is, but somehow uniquely unique. In fact, this 'uniqueness' simply played up differences with the West, which Japanese constantly pointed out to white foreigners, or *gaijin*. These ranged from daily customs (producing expressions of surprise and admiration when a *gaijin* managed to eat with chopsticks), to social organisation ('We Japanese operate in groups rather than as individuals'), to condescending explanations for the success of the Japanese economy before the 1990s (westerners lacked the Japanese work ethic and spirit of cooperation, which is why the European and US economies were going down the tubes, while Japan roared into the future). The theory of Japanese uniqueness – *nihonjinron* – spawned shelves full of books attempting to define the Japanese in terms of one or more of these 'unique' characteristics. Whether the expression was quaint or patronising, the vast majority of Japanese had learned to believe that the crucial truth about them was their fundamental difference from the rest of the world – and especially from westerners. Who were the Japanese? They were not *gaijin*.

At the end of the eighties and beginning of the nineties, however, these myths started to crumble. More Japanese travelled abroad, and not just on package tours but with backpacks. It became standard for young Japanese from a certain background to spend a year of high school or college overseas, usually in America. And while the economy flopped and destroyed bubble-era myths of an innate superiority at business, the Japanese were also now rich enough to dump the inferiority complex at the root of the 'uniqueness' nonsense. They were ready for a more normal means to express national pride.

But what? The imperial family remained mostly in the

background of national life, and the right seemed to have hijacked the most obvious national symbols. The red sun flag adorned ultra-nationalist sound trucks. The national anthem *Kimi ga yo* was especially controversial. A tenth-century poem put to a sombre tune, its words were almost unintelligible to modern Japanese. But they were generally interpreted to consist of a plea for the Emperor to reign forever. The Emperor had been stripped of all political powers at the end of World War Two, because abuse of a political system with Emperor Hirohito at its head had dragged Japan into that war in the first place. Whether or not to use the flag and anthem at school graduation ceremonies had long been controversial, and only in 1999 were they given official status.

When Japan qualified for the France World Cup, support for the national football team arrived to fill this vacuum – and enabled ordinary people to enjoy their flag and anthem. Before the final qualifying round, the Ultras had taken a huge Japanese flag – 17 metres long and 13 high – on a national tour, getting fans and even players to write messages and sign their names on it. They unfurled this over the stands before matches, and shook it in time with the 'Ni-ppon' chant. This wasn't easy for everyone, though. A writer in the weekly magazine *Sapio*, Koichi Yamazaki, described how watching the national team forced him to wrestle with his conscience over the patriotism he used to keep hidden. One voice in his head accused, 'You stood up when the national anthem played at the pre-match ceremony! In fact, you sang along.' Another countered, 'I didn't! I would never sing that anthem!' In the end he concluded morosely, 'It is a really sad person who can't support his own national team without going through this ridiculous self-interrogation and self-justification.'

Japanese football seemed a healthy enough version of patriotism. When jubilant fans making V-for-victory signs crossed the causeway bridge from Johor Bahru to Singapore after their victory over Iran, it was the first time any

Japanese had dared carry their flag there since 1942. Then the imperial army was marching into Singapore after conquering the Malay Peninsula. In 1997, they had been joined by thousands of Malaysians wishing them luck. The Ultras showed none of the xenophobia that plagued other national football teams. Instead, they were relentlessly good-humoured, respecting opponents' national anthems, and going round trying to make friends. In the games before the World Cup, they got in the mood for France by chanting, 'Oh la la / Oh la la / Oh la la Ni-ppon!' To drum up goodwill with their World Cup hosts, they recorded a version of a French pop song that had been a big hit in Japan several decades earlier, changing Michel Polnareff's lyrics from '*Tout, tout pour ma chérie, ma chérie*' to '*Allez, allez, allez, Japon!*' This was duly added to the repertoire of songs they sang during matches till the end of the World Cup.

After qualifying, Japan was put in a group with Argentina, Croatia and Jamaica, and a nationwide rush for tickets started as committed fans were joined by the newly converted. The Japan Travel Bureau chartered a plane for a three-day-no-night tour to see the Argentina game on Sunday, 14 June, leaving Japan at 11 p.m. on the Saturday, and arriving twelve hours later at dawn in Toulouse. After the match that afternoon participants would then fly straight back to Japan after just seventeen hours in France. The 312 places for the 255,000-yen (around £1,400) trip sold out in a day. Other tours spanning two weeks and taking in all three of Japan's matches sold for over 700,000 yen (nearly £4,000). Japan Airlines laid on an extra fourteen flights to Paris during the competition.

Team manager Okada knew the enthusiasm was not born simply of a love for football. 'The Japanese basically have an inferiority complex,' he said later. 'So people want to get over this by holding hands together and saying, "We are fantastic", or they start believing they can bring about a kamikaze,' – the divine wind that miraculously prevented the Mongols from invading Japan in the thirteenth century, and was later used to describe suicide pilots in World War Two. 'The Ultras were not about overcoming this inferiority complex. But the media and the rest of the nation were like this.'

TV-viewing figures for Japan's World Cup matches were the highest recorded for a live sports event since the rating system was introduced. A spectacular 67.3 per cent of Japanese watched the first match against Argentina, and 66.9 per cent tuned in for the Croatia game. In France, a mix-up over tickets meant that tour operators didn't have tickets for customers who had paid for tours to see the Argentina match. Hundreds abandoned their trips at the last minute, while others went to Toulouse and stood with signs saying '*Recherchez les billets*'. With touts rumoured to be selling tickets for as much as £4,000, almost none of the ticket seekers had any luck. As kick-off neared, some young Japanese women could be seen crying in the streets. Even about two hundred of the core group of Ultras had no tickets, so their tour operator provided thirty million yen (about £150,000) in French francs and US dollars for them to buy tickets off touts and French ticket holders.

In France, the Japanese fans displayed impeccable good manners. The thousands of Japanese who gathered in Toulouse seemed to watch in a mixture of bemusement and envy as Argentines carried flags round Toulouse singing and chanting. They still only felt comfortable making a noise when safely inside the stadium. In the town, they smiled back at the Argentines, shook hands, and sometimes exchanged shirts. The evening after the match, supporters from the two countries played a five-a-side game in Toulouse's central square, the Place du Capitole. After each of their matches, Japanese fans stayed behind and cleared up all the confetti they had thrown in the air at kick-off. In Lyons, where Japan played Jamaica, French stewards stood and watched in amazement at this behaviour, which was unheard of in European football history. When all the rubbish was packed into blue plastic bags and stacked at the stadium entrances, the stewards stood in line and applauded.

Japan's results in France – three straight losses – were matched for awfulness only by the USA team. For sure, the content of the first two games hadn't been that bad. Japan held the Argentine attack at bay for most of the game, slipping up only when Gabriel Batistuta pounced on a bad pass on the edge of the penalty area, and slotted the ball past the helpless Kawaguchi. Against Croatia they held out until seventy-seven minutes before succumbing to a Davor Suker goal and losing 1–0.

The Jamaica match, however, was an unhappy sight. Japan lost 2–1, with Nakayama only pulling back a consolation goal with sixteen minutes remaining. The sorriest figure of all was that of Shoji Jo, who had been picked out by manager Takeshi Okada as the key striker, the team's 'ace'. Unlike Nakayama and Kazu, Japan's proven forwards, Jo was young, having just turned twenty-three. He had gained in experience rapidly over the past two years, playing in the Atlanta Olympics and many of the World Cup qualifying games. He was fast and skilful, shooting well from both feet and with his head. If anyone could match the likes of Nakata and Kawaguchi as representatives of the future, it was Jo.

But in France he was clearly nervous. On one occasion against Croatia, he received the ball inside the opposition penalty area in plenty of space, but instead of turning to shoot, tried an overhead kick, which floated softly across the goal and wide of the far post. Later, after easily out-jumping a Croatian defender for a cross, he headed several metres off target. Against Jamaica, Jo was not only Japan's best hope of a goal, he was virtually required to score against these weakest of opponents, a team that had been partly cobbled together from English players with Jamaican roots and had already lost 5–0 to Argentina. But the expectation to score got to Jo's head. At one point he received the ball in the penalty area in plenty of space with no one between him and the goalkeeper. Though he had time to trap the ball and slide it coolly past the goalie, he instead volleyed it off target. Later, he trapped the ball quickly and neatly just outside the goal area – but then hoofed it miles over the bar.

All these were chances he would have done more with – probably scored in fact – if he had been playing for his club Yokohama Marinos, or if Japan had been playing in an Asian competition or any kind of friendly match. But in the World Cup Jo choked, and after each muffed shot he covered his face with his hands and turned his head to the sky. When he took his hands away, he revealed a big, embarrassed grin. As the team arrived back in Tokyo and filed through the airport, an irate fan threw water in Jo's face to let him know what he thought of his efforts. Jo, too, was unimpressed with himself. In spite of jet lag and the long flight from Europe, he went straight from the airport to the Marinos training ground, where he beat out his frustration by taking several hundred practice shots.

Interviewed on TV a few weeks later, Jo looked nervous as he tried to explain the problem. Rivulets of sweat poured down his face, and he wiped them away as he relived the hurt. 'It was a big stage,' he said, 'and the first time I'd been called the team's ace and expected to perform in that kind of match. Before you play football, you have to know yourself and have mental strength.'

CHAPTER TEN

Trouble

As the World Cup campaign fizzled, Japanese football was fast developing problems of a potentially far more damaging nature than poor finishing. In Johor Bahru, as the Japan team and staff started a lap of honour to celebrate their victory over Iran, hero of the moment Hidetoshi Nakata, exhausted and never a great one for celebrations anyway, had headed back alone to the dressing room. The national team's home games had been sold out throughout the qualifying campaign. But back at his club Hiratsuka Bellmare, he had played that season in front of crowds that averaged less than 8,000, no matter that the team also contained South Korea's Hong Myung-bo, probably Asia's best defender, and that visitors included world-class players like Dunga and Stojkovic. So when a reporter pointed a microphone at him, expecting expressions of pride and joy at having qualified for France, Nakata said: 'Everyone got excited about the World Cup. Now please come to watch the J.League.'

The J.League's early success had been reassuring to founders like Kawabuchi who had worried whether football would catch on in Japan. But the popularity had a bubble-like quality, much like that which had pushed Japanese share prices to silly levels a few years earlier. Then, because stocks were rising, they clearly had to be a good buy; so people decided to purchase them, and this demand meant that prices did indeed rise. After the initial spark of publicity that had made the J.League popular, people thought it must be worth seeing; so they went along, and spectator numbers grew to an extent that the crowds themselves did indeed make a spectacle worth seeing. For the first two or three years, the only limit on attendance was stadium size, as clubs had to make do with their 15,000 to 20,000 capacity stadiums for most matches. But any team that booked the National Stadium hauled in a near-full house of 50,000 for even the dullest encounter. Average attendance at J.League matches in 1993 was 17,976, and rose in 1994 to 19,598.

Around the end of 1995, however, Japan's enthusiasm for football began to wane. The people who had queued for hours just to watch any J.League game had now seen one. Teenage girls who had packed stadiums, shrieked at their favourite players, and splashed out on J.League accessories, found other things to pique their interest – like the *tamagotchi* virtual pet, and 'print club' machines that made your photo into stickers. Young men who might have supported their local clubs often became international football aficionados. They thought the J.League wasn't quite good enough and preferred to watch European football instead on satellite TV, and debate the merits of the English, German and Italian games. Some travelled all the way to Europe to watch games, and the football publications *Soccer Magazine* and *Soccer Digest* always carried advertisements for Serie A and Premier League package tours, taking in a number of prime matches over several days. While J.League attendance fell, the Toyota Intercontinental Cup, which offered the chance to see brand-name stars in Tokyo, sold out every year. When Manchester United played Palmeiras in 1999, thousands of Japanese turned up in United shirts, mostly with David Beckham's number seven on the back. When Beckham took corners, camera flashes lit up the National Stadium like Christmas lights. In Japanese parks and schoolyards, kick-around games featured an array of international replica shirts, from Flamengo to France, Roma to Real Madrid, and Argentina to Arsenal – but almost never a J.League shirt.

Influenced by the J.League, baseball updated its own image and a new breed of player emerged. Ichiro Suzuki, a laid-back outfielder with chiselled features, usually travelled in grungy cotton trousers and T-shirt rather than blazer and tie. Hideki Matsui, nicknamed Godzilla, declared he would strip naked if his Tokyo Giants team failed to win the 1996 pennant. Pitcher Hideo Nomo began a successful run with the Los Angeles Dodgers, convincing Japanese that they were better at the game than they had thought. Baseball revived and consolidated its status as Japan's number one spectator sport.

The earlier excitement over the J.League was starting to look like another of the crazes the Japanese call 'booms'. Once the novelty had worn off, what was there left to watch football for? Encouraged by the positive early response, Kawabuchi quickly increased the number of teams in the league, from ten in 1993 to eighteen in 1998. But with the entry of too many weak sides, match quality slipped. In April 1998, Masashi Nakayama of Jubilo Iwata scored a hat trick or more in each of four successive matches – one tally of five goals, two fours and a three – earning himself a place in the *Guinness Book of Records*. Five other players also scored hat tricks that month. Six or seven goals became common in J.League score lines. But instead of being entertaining, too many of these matches were so farcically one-sided they were dull.

Another problem was the Japanese dislike of confrontation and their unwillingness to compete aggressively. The good manners and reined-in egos that lubricated daily life in Japan did not make for good contests on the football field, and few J.League games were played with the kind of urgency seen in Europe and South America. This was partly down to a lack of incentives: until a second division was introduced in 1999, a team not in the title chase had nothing to play for – no Champions League or UEFA Cup places for the top few runners-up like in Europe, and no relegation for the weaker teams. Neither did many fans care too much whether they won or lost. At its launch, the J.League had drawn a sharp line between itself and the dreary old Japan Soccer League to form a strong brand identity. But this worked almost too well, and lots of fans ended up identifying with the league rather than their clubs. With no history of inter-team rivalries, they were 'J.Leaguers' before they were Flügels or Verdy supporters, and they saw other teams' followers as comrades instead of rivals – as seen in the unbearably friendly pre-game chants of the other team's name.

Kashima Antlers' In.Fight fans strongly opposed this pleasantness. They ignored friendship chants from opposing supporters and produced a CD of provocative songs with aggressive lyrics – 'Antlers! Antlers! Send them into a sea of blood!' They demanded fans be segregated at their home games, not in order to decrease tension as in Europe – there was rarely any actual fighting – but to *increase* it by creating a feeling of us against them. Similarly, Urawa Reds imported an extending tunnel from Italy to shield players from missiles as they walked out on to the pitch. There was no actual need for the tunnel, but such protection enhanced the mood by hinting at potential violence. In.Fight leader Kawazu defended pitch invasions, and wrote in his fanzine column that it was OK to throw things onto the field, so long as you were prepared to get arrested. The club received dozens of letters of complaint, but Kawazu thought his stand was essential: people went to football matches – rather than watching on TV, where you can see better – for the atmosphere, which is created by tension, of which there was not enough. 'The Japanese like it when everyone is friends, but this kills the interest of sport,' he said. 'I wanted to destroy the cosiness and raise the tension. If you don't cause trouble, the J.League won't generate the right mood.'

Killing the mood further were the terrible decisions by local governments – who owned the grounds rather than the clubs – to build new stadiums with running tracks. When the town of Kashiwa built a six-billion-yen (£40 million) new stadium for Reysol, the fans hated it. The old ground had no roof and was small, fitting just 15,000 spectators at a squeeze. But it was a convenient fifteen-minute walk from Kashiwa's main station, and offered a close-up view of the pitch. The smart new stadium seated 20,000 under roofs, and its elegant design included flood-lights on tall poles that leaned over the stadium at an angle. But it had a running track, and was located in a park development out of town, which had insufficient parking space for cars and was a thirty-minute trip from central Kashiwa by train and bus. The fans protested at the first game there, holding up banners saying, 'Hard to see, hard to get to – we don't recognise this as our home stadium.' They booed the mayor and threw fifty red smoke bombs on to the track (they couldn't find any their own colour, yellow).

Warned afterwards that smoke bombs were not allowed and that their use could lead to new security measures for the league, the supporters stayed away from the next home game (held at the old ground) as an act of penitence. But a month later, the second game in the new stadium erupted into a worse-tempered protest, intensified by Reysol's losing 1–0 to Verdy. Normally the fans stayed behind after each game to pick up the scraps of newspaper used for kick-off confetti. This time, they threw it all on to the running track, along with plastic bottles, paper beer cups and anything else they could find. A strong wind blew most of the rubbish into the water jump, half filling it. A few supporters went over to abuse a TV cameraman whose crane they claimed had obstructed their view of the game. When security guards blocked their way, a fight broke out. It only ended when supporters' leader Yoichi Yamamoto, seeing that a line had been crossed, picked up his megaphone and said calmly, '*Shuryo, shuryo*' – 'That's enough, that's enough.'

A few years later, the twenty brand-new stadiums built in Japan and South Korea for 2002 made up the biggest array of new sports arenas ever constructed for a World Cup. Some of the gleaming, metallic arenas featured arched roofs that bent gracefully over the stands, and one – the Sapporo Dome – looked like a giant mercury bubble. They functioned flawlessly. But while seven out of ten of the

Korean grounds were designed just for football, only three of Japan's were – Kobe plus the football-savvy towns of Urawa (which later became part of Saitama) and Kashima. (Though it had no track, the Sapporo Dome was an indoor arena and was designed also to host baseball games on artificial grass. A natural turf pitch slid in on a bed of air for football. The northern city built a dome because it is snowbound for much of the winter. But in June, the month of the World Cup, it has by far the most pleasant climate of any of the host cities – cool and dry, while the rest of Japan is either boiling hot or awash with rain.) The reason for these atmosphere-crushing stadiums was that local governments wanted to use them for Japan's National Athletic Meet, which travels to a different prefecture each year, and is a source of central government grants. This athletic meet usually attracted a full house on just one day, that of the opening ceremony. The rest of the year, domestic track and field played almost no part in Japanese life as a spectator sport. The people who made these decisions were old, not much interested in football and, if they ever went to a game, watched from grandstand seats along the side of the pitch. They had no idea what it was like to watch from ground level, forty metres behind the goal, and to have to catch the TV highlights later to find out how goals had been scored at the far end.

For all these reasons, Japan's football stadiums gradually became quieter, and by late 1997, average J.League attendance had dipped below 10,000. The league appeared to be dying off, and it looked as though Japan and domestic league football simply didn't mix. But a closer look showed that, after the early J.League hubbub had died down, the Japanese followed football teams for much the same reasons as people everywhere else. Clubs that understood the chemistry thrived. The others flopped. At one extreme, on the rainy night of 14 October 1998, Vissel Kobe recorded a J.League record low of 2,091 spectators sprinkled around its 60,000-seat concrete stadium. At the other, Urawa's Komaba stadium was packed with 20,000 people for every

Reds home game, and thousands of people were on a waiting list for season tickets. Managers of other clubs – including Verdy, JEF Ichihara and Hiratsuka Bellmare – called the Reds management office and asked Hitoshi Sato: What is the secret?

Sato told them it was down to a lot of little things, like the match-day programme and the official supporters club, which had forged a sense of belonging for the people of Urawa: nearly five thousand supporters clubs were listed in the annual *Urawa Reds Official Handbook*, with names like 'The Grand Red', 'Red Buddy' and 'Paint It Red'. While the club created this environment, instead of trying to entertain the crowd and force the support, it left the fans to lead themselves on the terraces. While the hard-core supporters made themselves heard on the terraces, a Reds back-up group led by local government officials and businessmen provided stewards, and arranged trips to away matches for families and older people, thus giving the whole town a way to get involved in the club. The team became an essential part of a town that functioned as a Tokyo commuter suburb and had little else to distinguish itself. Urawa residents no longer told people in other parts of Japan they were from near Tokyo; they could now say 'Urawa' when asked, and everyone knew it as the Reds' hometown.

Kashima, too, was another anonymous town before the Antlers won several J.League championships. Understanding the need to give supporters a voice in club affairs, the Antlers let In.Fight leader Kawazu write his controversial fanzine column from an office in the Antlers' clubhouse. He resigned as supporters' leader in 1998, deciding the Antlers crowd no longer needed to be goaded along. Instead, he ran in a town council election as a football-friendly independent candidate, calling for parks and streets to be named after Antlers players, and for game results to be announced over the town's natural-disaster-warning system. He was elected comfortably.

Verdy should have been one of the J.League's great

popular successes. It had a proud history as Yomiuri Club, Japan's first big football team organised like a club. As well as a Japan Soccer League team, other people could play and train at its facilities in suburban Tokyo. And in the days of corporate amateurism, Yomiuri's players alone were not company employees with jobs for life: if their contracts were not renewed, they had to find work elsewhere. But the *Yomiuri* newspaper had been determined that stars and samba would turn it into an elite team. Verdy rode the early J.League boom like no other club, winning the first two championships and attracting the highest average home attendance for the first three years. But Yomiuri didn't show much respect for Kawasaki, the hometown it had reluctantly chosen because no appropriate stadium had been available in Tokyo. Late in 1993, Verdy announced a plan to switch locations to become Tokyo Verdy rather than Kawasaki Verdy – the team of the capital rather than a dull town of commuter housing and industry. The J.League quashed the plan as a violation of its hometown principle, but the insult registered. When the J.League Division Two began, another Kawasaki team, Frontale, pulled in nearly as many spectators as Verdy despite only being in J2. Frontale taunted Verdy with a slogan on posters at the local station: 'Kawasaki Frontale – a football team born in Kawasaki'.

Then Verdy's fans split into factions and started quarrelling, and the club owners soon saw something was wrong. At the end of 1996, Camisa Doze leader Yamaguchi told several newspapers and magazines that he thought new Brazilian manager Emerson Leao was useless. The club management used this as an excuse to abolish Camisa Doze as the official supporters group. 'Their attitude was that they didn't need supporters,' said Yamaguchi. 'So I said OK, we won't support any more.' In 1997 Kawasaki's Todoroki stadium began to empty, and by 1999, crowds often numbered under 5,000, down from Verdy's average of more than 20,000 in the early days. In one corner of the home stand, about a hundred supporters calling themselves the Kawasaki Hearts did their best, decking the terrace with green and white strips of nylon and banging drums and singing. In another, a rump group of half a dozen samba lovers played on. The two groups talked occasionally about supporting together, but could never quite reach an agreement.

In their desperation to liven up the atmosphere, Verdy's owners added more gimmicks. The public-address system started making announcements in Portuguese as well as Japanese, even though few Brazilians could be seen in the stands. And they gave the players official nicknames, which were read out before matches with the team line-up: 'Bomber Head' (for a player with a big perm), 'Elite Hunter' (a striker), and 'Bronco of the Wing'. None of this helped, and in late 1999 the owners again applied to do what they had tried to do six years earlier – move the club to Tokyo. This time, seeing the team's plight, the J.League agreed, and the move was set for 2001. Tsunayoshi Ota, the leader of the Kawasaki Hearts, was disgusted at the betrayal of his town after his years of support. 'They don't love me,' he decided, 'so I'm not going to love them.' He became a Frontale supporter instead.

Fewer football fans meant less money. While the diminishing turn-outs reduced gate receipts, club revenues were hit further as the perks of the J.League boom vanished. First, the J.League brand lost its appeal. Fees collected from licensed goods shrank from 3.6 billion yen (£20 million) in 1993 to 470 million (less than £3 million) in 1997, as cuddly mascots went out of fashion and fans decided they didn't need a new replica shirt every year. In addition, football didn't agree with Japanese TV-watching habits. Instead of concentrating on the box, the Japanese more often like to have the television on in the background to fill silences or provide conversation topics. Baseball worked well in this context because of its frequent breaks. But football demanded intense concentration throughout the game. It also made it hard to show advertisements, and live match broadcasts were often interrupted mid-game for commercial breaks. Gradually, Japan's TV networks removed football from primetime.

Despite their smaller revenues, J.League teams kept on spending. Because the J.League was too young to have an established hierarchy of small, medium and large clubs, all seemed to think that early cash outlays would help attract fans and turn them into one of the big ones. As their home cities built new arenas in anticipation that the boom would continue or even gain momentum, the clubs threw money at brand-name foreign stars in order to stay with the competition. When USA '94 top scorer Hristo Stoitchkov came to Japan in 1998, he completed – with Gary Lineker (1986) and Salvatore Schillacci (1990) – a hat trick of Golden Boot winners. Some of the money was well spent. The warrior football of Brazil's Jorginho (130 million yen – about £800,000 – a year) and Dunga (160 million – almost £1 million) inspired their teams to championship wins. But the high salaries encouraged a more general wage inflation. Dunga's teammate Nakayama was paid 90 million yen (about £500,000), and Japan captain Ihara 100 million (about £600,000), even though both would have struggled to make the team at most first division European clubs. In 1998, Verdy's four top Japanese players were still paid over 90 million yen (£500,000) each, even though they had been dropped from the national team. The league estimated some clubs had a salary bill 70 per cent of their total revenues, compared to a level of 45 per cent normal at the time in most European leagues. Chairman Kawabuchi described this as 'a ridiculously high figure by world standards'.

The first sign of the trouble this was causing came from Shimizu S-Pulse. S-Pulse was different from the J.League's other founding members. Shimizu had a richer football tradition than any other city in Japan. Shimizu high schools regularly won the national championship, and more professionals came from Shimizu than anywhere else in the country. So when the J.League began, a group of local businessmen decided they could form a club by themselves instead of inviting a company team to set up there. S-Pulse's founders set up a holding company called S-Rap, and persuaded TV Shizuoka, a local TV station, to put up most of the money. They also gathered support from local businesses and over a thousand townspeople, who paid 100,000 or 200,000 yen (£600 or £1,200) each to become shareholders. They then persuaded locally bred players with company teams to come home and play for their town. As the only J.League club that had not originated in a company team, S-Pulse was a model for Kawabuchi's vision of sport in the community.

But when the J.League boom ended, S-Pulse had no corporate backer to fall back on. Following the trend elsewhere in Japan, average attendance fell from 22,910 in the second half of 1994, to 9,537 in the 1997 second stage. S-Rap had made the same mistake as other clubs in overspending, and brought in top foreigners, like former Italy captain Daniele Massaro, as well as building a new training ground. By 1997 it had lost a cumulative total of two billion yen (£13 million). Activist fans worried about the club's survival, and collected money to buy an orange car with loudspeakers, which they drove round town publicising matches. But in November 1997 S-Rap announced that main shareholder TV Shizuoka would inject no new money, and S-Pulse faced collapse. The club was only saved after fans collected 300,000 signatures and persuaded a local industrial group to take over.

Other J.League clubs had rich owners who could pad their accounts with handouts. J.League figures showed that the total contribution from sponsors – in most cases the owners – nearly doubled, from 2.3 billion yen (about £13 million) in 1993 to 4.1 billion (nearly £26 million) in 1997. But even this could not last. The league had been conceived in 1989, at the height of Japan's financial bubble when corporations were awash with cash. And it had been born in 1993, when Japan thought its mighty economy was just hitting a speed bump. But by the late 1990s, it had become clear that Japan had shifted down a gear for good.

Moreover, the political changes in the air in 1993 had also begun to appear illusory. By 1997, the old guard of Liberal Democratic Party politicians had outfoxed the youngish reformers who had taken over four years earlier, and were back in charge with their usual goal: to make sure Japan changed only at a snail's pace, lest its supporters in farming and the construction industry suffered. The economy sagged into recession, and the national debt swelled as the government tried to spend its way out of the slump. Soon, for the first time in over half a century, millions of Japanese workers found themselves unemployed. Some football club owners numbered among Japan's – and the world's – greatest industrial titans. Hitachi owned Kashiwa Reysol, Toyota owned Nagoya Grampus Eight, and Matsushita (maker of the Panasonic and National brands) owned Gamba Osaka. They could still write off their teams' losses and barely notice the difference. But the rest began scrambling to cut costs.

Yokohama Flügels had all the standard J.League problems and then some. The fans had long since split into factions and with the constant bickering in the stands, the Flügels had never developed the kind of crowd seen at Urawa. Too many of the fans they attracted at the start turned out to be of a more fickle variety. Gert Engels, a German who was the club's head coach for several years, remembered the players joking about the girls who came every day to watch training: 'Who's she coming for?' they said. 'That one's yours, isn't she? She's here again today.' But when a player left – like midfield favourite Masakiyo Maezono, who went to Verdy – the girls left too. 'The girls are focused on the boys, not on the game,' Engels said. 'If a player marries or a girl marries, then the girls go away.'

In 1998, the Flügels began using the new 70,000-seat Yokohama International Stadium, which had been built for the 2002 World Cup final. Curiosity in the new facility, along with a cut in ticket prices and schemes that amounted to giving away thousands of tickets, boosted the Flügels' average attendance to nearly 16,000. But unlike the old

Yokohama ground, the 15,000-seat Mitsuzawa, which felt full enough with about 10,000 present, the huge new stadium felt miserable even with the larger number. It also had a running track, which added to the feeling of emptiness and reduced some spectators to using binoculars for a better view, while others switched their attention between the pitch and the big screen where portions of the game were broadcast simultaneously. Yokohama International also cost the club more in rent and staff: a game at Mitsuzawa was said to break even with just 6,000 paying spectators; Yokohama International needed 22,000. The Flügels could not back out though, because the city had built the new stadium on the understanding – established when the J.League was booming – that the team would use it for most home matches. Adding to this financial burden the Flügels had a hefty salary bill, including packages worth more than 100 million yen (nearly £600,000) for international players like Brazilian midfielder Cesar Sampaio and Japan's Motohiro Yamaguchi. By this time, the Flügels' owners were suffering from other problems too: All Nippon Airways' non-core businesses like hotels were losing money; Sato Kogyo, the construction company, had been losing money for several years because public-sector construction projects had dried up. Early in 1998, Sato told ANA that it could no longer afford its share of the annual 1.5 billion yen (£9 million) the two companies paid towards the football team.

ANA officials later claimed to have tried in vain to find a new partner. They never said whom they were supposed to have approached, and no company ever said that ANA had come asking it for help in running the Flügels. In short, no evidence ever came to light that such a search had taken place. However, one company ANA did speak to was Nissan Motor, owner of Yokohama's other team, the Marinos. Hard times in Japan had forced corporations to take previously unthinkable measures. Nissan had built too many factories in the go-go era and could no longer sell enough cars. In 1998 the company made a loss, sold off its headquarters building in downtown Tokyo, and was looking for a partner to inject funds – a plea later answered when Renault of France took a large stake and installed a Brazilian-French chief executive officer. This pattern was starting all over Japan, especially in banks and securities houses, which were merging so they could pool customers while reducing their cost base. And if car companies could form alliances and banks could merge, why shouldn't a pair of football teams do the same?

CHAPTER ELEVEN

The People's Club

Yokohama Flügels were having an average season till the club was abolished. They had come eighth out of eighteen in the 1998 first stage, and were stuck in mid-table in the second. With three Japan internationals and Sampaio, a member of Brazil's runner-up side in the France World Cup, they should have done better. But Spanish manager Carles Rexach Serda, a former coach (and future manager) of Barcelona, had not gelled with the players, and his attempts to make them play like his old club had resulted in a run of defeats. In September, however, Rexach had been fired, and the team was finding its rhythm under the former head coach, Gert Engels. With three straight wins followed by a careless loss, the team mood was rising.

For the playing staff, the news arrived like a malicious rumour, bouncing round Yokohama by telephone on the night of 28 October. The next morning the story was on the front page of every newspaper in Japan and at the top of every TV bulletin. The Flügels were going to merge with the Marinos, Yokohama's other team. It wasn't an equal merger, though – Marinos owner Nissan would have a 70 per cent stake in the new club, while the Flügels majority owner All Nippon Airways would take 30 per cent. The new club would be called Yokohama F Marinos, and there would be just a handful of slots for Flügels players. In reality the Flügels were being swallowed up. The first official notice to the players was a piece of paper explaining the deal that was handed to them when they arrived at the clubhouse. Three executives from ANA Sports addressed a meeting. 'I expect you know from TV and the papers, but we're merging,' said company president Tsunehiko Yamada. 'If any of you have questions . . .'

No players changed for the regular 9.30 training session, and Engels said any players who wanted could miss the afternoon session. At 2 p.m., however, they all came back. Engels told them to play a mini-game because it was impossible to focus on regular drills. They played in silence, without the usual talking and shouting. One player got kicked badly, and left the field dragging his bruised left leg behind him. It had been an accident. No one could concentrate on football.

The day after the announcement, twenty Flügels fans visited the J.League headquarters in central Tokyo and handed chairman Kawabuchi a written appeal to freeze the merger. League rules meant the two clubs needed approval from the governing body before the merger could go through. Kawabuchi had asked the Flügels and Marinos presidents whether they couldn't find other sponsors or start with a smaller-scale club even if it meant dropping to the new J2, but they simply told him their superiors had made the decision. Kawabuchi had decided that the merger was a lesser evil than if Nissan and ANA withdrew from football completely, and he approved the deal. But when the Flügels supporters told Kawabuchi how upset they were, he broke down in tears. 'I didn't know you cared so much,' he told them, and then added: 'I can't lead this, but if you collected several hundred thousand signatures, something might change.'

Football mergers are proposed elsewhere from time to time. But usually, an idea is floated, supporters from both sides protest, and the plan is shelved. Something like this happened with Reading and Oxford United in 1983, and later with Queen's Park Rangers and first Fulham, then Wimbledon. Cities like Dundee and Sheffield, which might sustain one big, competitive club, prefer to continue with two weaker teams because that's the way the supporters like it.

That's also the way Yokohama supporters would have liked it, despite the short history of their clubs. But the owners hadn't even thought to ask. They appeared to have no idea of how the J.League was supposed to be different from their old corporate sports teams. Kawabuchi had dreamed of sports clubs throughout the nation to serve as a focus for communities, where families would support their local team. The owners still thought they were running a sideline business that might raise their corporate image. ANA jettisoned the Flügels as if they had decided to abandon an unprofitable air route, thinking passengers would be happy to fly rival Japan Airlines instead.

The first sign that the Flügels management had misjudged the likely reaction came the following Saturday. Before the game they showed a video retrospective of the club's history on the giant screen at Yokohama International Stadium. Catching a glimpse of this as they walked into the stadium, the players were furious: first the owners had abolished the club without warning; now they were using it as material for pre-match entertainment. They went out and thumped Cerezo Osaka 7–0, scoring a league record five goals in the first half. Even Sergio Etsugo, a Japanese–Brazilian who was Japan's most acid-tongued football critic, wrote that he was moved to tears by the result.

What's more, the fans woke up for the first time in months. They had met up before the match to try and work together for the first time in nearly six years and throughout, they banged drums and waved dozens of blue and white flags. After the game, they cheered as the players greeted them with arms raised in defiance. Later, ANA Sports president Yamada addressed a crowd of 1,200 remaining in the stands. The meeting started after the match, at around six in the evening, and was not really a discussion. The fans shouted that they wanted the merger cancelled. Yamada and other managers replied that they couldn't, and that the company had 'made the greatest possible efforts to avoid the merger', looking for new sponsors to inject cash into the club. When a company official pointed out that, 'if this number of people had come to watch every week, it would never have come to this,' one supporter had to be restrained from attacking him. At 10 o'clock the stadium management wanted to shut down for the night, so they moved to the car park. At 2.30 in the morning, Yamada finally agreed to let the fans meet officials from parent company ANA, and the fans agreed to go home.

This set the pattern for their contacts. The supporters demanded the merger be abandoned, and the company said no, just hearing them out in the hope they would let off steam and the episode would pass. Koji Maruo, the executive in charge of ANA's affiliated companies, met a group of sixty supporters and told them repeatedly that the merger was a final decision. When he told them the club had lost several hundred million yen in total, the supporters asked him to run the team on a cut-rate basis, as ANA was already planning to contribute 500 million yen a year to the new Yokohama F Marinos – more than the total budget of some of the teams preparing to enter J2. Why not continue the Flügels in J2? 'There is no point in running a team if it is not in J1,' Maruo replied. 'We don't know how much we would get in gate receipts in J2, and there is no merit in it for the company.'

Marinos supporters, even though they did not stand to suffer as much as the Flügels, had also reacted angrily to the merger. At their first match after the announcement, they put up a banner threatening, 'Kohsaka, Taniguchi [the club's president and managing director] – watch out!' When these two managers came to explain the merger, one fan threw a megaphone at Taniguchi's head, leaving him with a two-centimetre gash above the eye. 'Think of it as the pain in our hearts!' someone shouted after him.

But the Flügels supporters were generally peaceful, and they began a quiet, determined campaign to get their way. They were already one of the meekest crowds in the J.League, with a greater proportion of women and families than most other clubs, and cynics suggested this was the reason they were being swallowed up by the Marinos rather than the other way round. They also calculated that any hope of saving their club depended on their generating good will with the J.League, the JFA and sponsors. Crossing the line into violence would destroy this. Immediately after the merger announcement, some Flügels supporters had called their counterparts at S-Pulse in Shimizu to ask how they had helped save their club. The reply was a signature campaign, and the Flügels supporters did just this. Starting with the Cerezo Osaka game, they began to gather a petition against the merger, giving everyone who signed a blue ribbon to pin on their coat. Then they formed the 'Save the Flügels Group', and began a campaign of silent demonstrations and appeals, calling on everyone to avoid any 'heated' actions. When the team flew to Sapporo for the last J.League match of the season, a dozen supporters went to Tokyo's Haneda airport to see them off, and remained afterwards in the departure hall in front of an ANA counter. They wore replica uniforms, with blue ribbons on the left sleeve and the ANA logo blocked out with sticky tape, and held a banner calling for the preservation of the Flügels. The fans stood in silence for an hour, getting photographed for the papers, but giving airport officials no excuse to throw them out. The nearest they came to violence was on a visit to the ANA headquarters at Haneda. After a group of fans rushed to try to board a lift, a young woman supporter was knocked to the ground, spraining her left ankle. In the minor ruckus that followed, one supporter broke a ceramic ashtray.

As well as quiet protests, they issued a series of polite appeals. They warned the mayor of Yokohama that as 'Yokohama is competing with Urawa to hold the 2002 World Cup final, if the city of Yokohama destroys this community culture through the Flügels, it will invite the opposition of all football fans and be a big minus.' Supporters of most other J.League clubs had helped their signature campaign (as well as chanting 'Yokohama Flügels!' at unrelated matches), and by mid-December about a third of a million people had signed. Delivering these to Kawabuchi at the J.League, the Save the Flügels Group flattered the chairman with the words: 'We think the 346,050 signatures are proof that a new community ... is producing a kind of culture that did not exist before in Japan. ... This culture has grown from the seeds that Chairman Kawabuchi sowed with the J.League.' They were even respectful towards ANA: 'It was fantastic that you decided to form a football club ... rooted in the local community, and thereby as one of Japan's leading airlines carried out your responsibility as a corporate citizen,' read one protest note, before continuing: 'But [the merger] was a betrayal of the thanks and expectations soccer fans felt towards your company.'

The Flügels played their last home match on 7 November. After this they had one more away game in the J.League, followed by the post-season Emperor's Cup, which was played in different locations round Japan. So the last game at Yokohama's Mitsuzawa ground had an air of finality. The players posed for the pre-match photo covering with their right hands the ANA logo on their left sleeves, so their arms also hid the logos on their chests. The Flügels won 2–1, and at the final whistle several players collapsed in the centre circle. Fans were in tears. The sun set beautifully over the stadium, showing Mount Fuji in silhouette on the distant horizon. The players and staff then walked round the ground waving Flügels flags and carrying banners saying, 'Let's try together to save the club', 'Let's keep fighting together', and 'Help the Flügels'. Tears streamed down the cheeks of some of the players as they stayed behind to sign autographs. Several thousand supporters remained for yet another talk with the ANA Sports managers. The same three came out on to the pitch, and by now any pretence of reasoned debate was long gone. They set up a microphone half-way between the centre circle and penalty area and repeated that the merger would go ahead as planned. Then they shuffled off to shouts of '*Baka ni suru na yo*!' – 'Don't treat us like idiots!' Tamaki Kawamura, a leader of the largest Flügels support group Asa Azul, tried to explain what it was like to have your club abolished like this. Acknowledging that times were hard for both Yoko-hama clubs, she could still not buy the corporate logic that had driven the merger. 'For us it's like a family,' she said. 'If your dad gets fired from his job and you haven't got much money, then you simply don't eat as well as before. You don't get rid of Dad and merge with the family next door.'

The players had even less success than the fans in their attempts to influence ANA. The day after their 7–0 victory over Cerezo Osaka, they stood outside Yokohama Station with clipboards collecting signatures. One thousand people signed in fifteen minutes, before a station employee moved them on. So they looked for other ways to protest. They thought of boycotting their remaining games, but were warned they might face bans. They wanted to abandon flying ANA to away matches, but their contracts forced them to obey the team management's travel plans. They suggested a strike to the J.League Players Association, but the association said that this, too, would be against league regulations. Appealing to Kawabuchi, they came away simply with an assurance that they would be given free transfers.

With no idea how to save the club, the squad suffered mentally. Captain Motohiro Yamaguchi woke up in the middle of the night after dreams where he was playing in another club's uniform. Winger Atsuhiro Miura had a series of crying jags – not because he normally cried a lot, but because he hated losing and couldn't stand not being able to do anything. Koji Maeda got drunk and stayed drunk for three days after the announcement. He found it most painful when his daughter kept asking, 'Why are the Flügels disappearing?' and he didn't know how to explain. On 12 December all thirty-five Flügels players and staff – some of them in tears as they put pen to paper – signed an open letter to ANA's managers: 'We have judged that there is no point in continuing negotiations any longer with ANA, which has shown no sincerity. We think it is a great shame that we have played for an owner like this.'

But they were not yet finished. The Emperor's Cup took

place over the course of a month following the end of the J.League. Some Flügels players had floated the idea of boycotting the cup as a protest move. Others were worried that a serious injury in the cup might leave a player with no contract for the next year. Manager Engels had another idea, though. Throughout their weeks of despair, he had pressed the players to stay in shape for the cup, because a good run might help those who were less well known to find new clubs. Better still, it would serve as a kind of proof that the Flügels were too good a team to shut down, and so might help pull off a last-minute reprieve from somewhere. 'I want to show we are right by winning,' he told the squad. Either way, raising the Emperor's Cup aloft in a packed National Stadium on 1 January as millions of Japanese watched on TV while tucking into their New Year's lunches – that would be the ultimate act of defiance.

The Flügels started the Emperor's Cup nervously. Any game they lost would be their last, and this frightened rather than motivated the players. In their first two matches they struggled to victories against teams not even in the J.League. But after these, they relaxed. Against first-stage champions Jubilo Iwata, they took the lead after six minutes, when Miura found Sampaio with a long throw and the Brazilian flicked the ball on for Yoshikiyo Kuboyama to score with his left foot. Jubilo equalised in the middle of the second half, but Takayuki Yoshida then headed the winner – again from a Miura throw touched on by Sampaio. In the semi-finals they faced second-stage champions Kashima Antlers, whom they had lost to in the previous year's Emperor's Cup final. Again the Flügels got an early goal, this time after just three minutes, when the Antlers failed to clear a cross, and Hideki Nagai fired a thundering half-volley from outside the penalty area. They defended stubbornly, and by the end of the match they had secured their place in the cup final.

Though many Japanese had tired of the week-by-week routine of league football, they loved a good drama, especially a tearjerker like the one the proud, indignant

Flügels players were laying on. As this heroic cup run gathered momentum, the number of Flügels 'supporters' increased. By the time they played Jubilo and the Antlers, they had attracted so much attention that attendance was nearly double the typical number during the season norm – and this was for matches held in Kobe and Osaka, about 400 kilometres from Yokohama. Staff at the Flügels supporters' shop in Yokohama had worried after the merger announcement that they would not get rid of a new order of long warm-up coats that had just arrived. But during the last month sales jumped to five times their previous rate, and by the time it closed down in January nearly all the stock had sold out. The players suddenly found unprecedented crowds turning up to their regular training sessions, with five hundred watching the final public session on 30 December, two days before the team's final game. The players, who recognised supporters that came to watch regularly, tried to dodge requests for souvenir autographs from new fans who hadn't come earlier. 'Where were all these people,' Yamaguchi thought at the time. 'Why didn't they come to see us earlier?'

The Flügels' opponents for the final were Shimizu S-Pulse, the same as for their first ever J.League match. That game had been at home at Yokohama's Mitsuzawa ground on 16 May 1993. It had been packed, but up to three-quarters of the fans were from Shimizu as the Flügels had not yet figured how to create a fan base. On 1 January 1999, the ratio was reversed. About 20,000 S-Pulse fans painted one end of the stadium orange, but with every neutral fan in the country backing the Flügels, the rest of the ground was a mass of blue and white flags, shirts and banners. Ten minutes before kick-off, the Nippon Ultras floated one of their banners over the crowd: the image was of a shouting fan with the words, 'You'll never walk alone.'

S-Pulse were offering no sympathy. They had been saved by the efforts of fans just a year earlier, and a new toughness had taken them to the cup final for the first time. Now they wanted a reward for their hard work, and they came out attacking from the start. After thirteen minutes Teruyoshi Ito crossed from the right, and Masaaki Sawanobori met the ball with a diving header that beat goalie Seigo Narazaki and flew just inside the post. After this, S-Pulse kept running forward, looking like they would add another any time. The Flügels, hit once again by an attack of nerves, had their backs to the wall and were fighting to stay in the match. But in first-half injury time, Yoshikiyo Kuboyama pounced on a loose ball inside the penalty area and equalised. S-Pulse tired in the second half, allowing the Flügels to dominate. After seventy-three minutes, a long pass from Sampaio found Nagai just inside the S-Pulse penalty area. He trapped and threaded the ball across to Yoshida, who slotted the ball between two defenders and past the goalkeeper. The Flügels were 2–1 ahead.

Captain Yamaguchi wrote later that after this, he started thinking what he usually thought when leading a match: that there was not long to hold out. Just seventeen minutes to go and we've won, he thought. 'End quickly. End quickly . . .' The words repeated in his head. Fifteen minutes to go, ten, five . . . But when there were just five minutes left, he no longer wanted it to end, and the new words in his head were, 'Only five more minutes and it will all be over.' The thought even leapt up: 'If they score an equaliser we'll have extra time and I can keep playing in the Flügels uniform.'

At 3.23 the final whistle blew, and the Flügels had played their last football. The coaches, substitutes and the younger players who had not been on the pitch for a minute of the cup campaign – all rushed the pitch, jumping for joy, hugging each other and crying. Even the Shimizu fans chanted 'Yokohama Flügels!' The Flügels players walked over to them, lined up and took a bow. At the other end, they took off their shirts, boots and socks, and threw them into the stands.

Astonishingly, the Flügels' owners at ANA still appeared determined to pretend they had done nothing wrong and that they could ultimately save face. Before the final the players and staff had said that, whatever the result, they wanted a celebration or commiseration party for just their families. But when they arrived at the Yokohama Prince Hotel, they were greeted by a round of applause from ANA executives, most of whom they had never met. With another big round of applause, the players were directed to a stage. At first they refused to go up, but then an ANA official walked up to captain Yamaguchi, and asked him to make a toast. Normal Japanese toasts follow lengthy preliminary remarks – multiple thank-yous, reflections on what has gone before, and hopes for the future. Yamaguchi said just one word: '*Kampai*.' This means 'cheers', but spoken sullenly with no preambles, to a group of executives who had made sure the Flügels would never defend their trophy, it came across like an insult. Their act of defiance immaculately carried off, Yamaguchi and the players filed out to a separate room, where they had a party for their wives and kids.

When the new season started in March 1999, the F Marinos were not much different from the old Marinos. The team was almost unchanged, and contained only three former Flügels. The club badge, sailor-seagull emblem, and blue shirts, white shorts and red socks were the same as before – all that had changed was the presence of the letter 'F' in the club name. But their supporters were a lot unhappier, and disagreeing on how to deal with the merger, they split into two factions. The pragmatist group inserted the new name 'F Marinos' into the old support songs. The fundamentalist group sat through games in silent protest, and then mostly stopped turning up at all. The atmosphere at matches became quieter than before.

Some Flügels fans did not care very much that their club had vanished: they simply went off to follow whatever team their favourite player had joined, putting away their Flügels shirts and buying a replica of the new club's uniform. These seemed to demonstrate that J.League chairman Kawabuchi's ideas of sport for the community had drifted past a nation more interested in short-lived fashions. However, others had taken his message to heart. One of these, Tomio Tsujino, had followed professional wrestling and baseball as a boy, and never been interested in football. But when the J.League had started he was attracted by the foreign stars, as well as the idea that the league was the Japanese equivalent of other football leagues all over the world, making Japan part of a world sporting community. He had never joined a supporters group, and watched the Flügels' home games quietly from the side of the pitch rather than from behind the goal. So when the supporters wanted to unite behind a common cause, his neutrality made him an ideal leader for the Save the Flügels Group. Tsujino led this for several weeks and then, shortly after the merger was formally signed, made a statement on TV abandoning the campaign to stop it. The Save the Flügels Group became the 'Rebuild The Flügels Group', and began trying to set up a new club.

They set a target of 10 million yen (about £60,000), and began seeking individual donations of 10,000 yen (£60). By late December 1998, they had collected 67 million yen (£370,000), and filed an application to set up a new company. Nissan and ANA, apparently worried that the new club might steal support from the merged Yokohama F Marinos, refused to yield the name 'Flügels', so they called the new company Yokohama Fulie Sports Club, after an old nickname for the Flügels, and its team Yokohama FC.

They modelled the club on FC Barcelona, which is effectively a private members club, bankrolled by its supporters. 'Socio Fuliesta' charged members 30,000 yen (£200) a year, or 50,000 yen (£300) with a season ticket. By April 1999, 2,200 people had joined – not the 10,000 they needed to cover running costs, but enough for a start. Sport management company IMG offered to raise money from sponsors for low consulting fees in exchange for a cut of accessories such as replica shirts, and brought on board sponsors including Citibank and Bosch. IMG also introduced them to former Bundesliga player Yasuhiko Okudera and Pierre Littbarski, who became general manager and team manager respectively. Most important of all, the only people who could decide to close down Yokohama Fulie Sports Club were the supporters themselves.

Though its lack of experience barred Yokohama FC from immediately entering the J.League, it was allowed to play with the corporate and university teams that made up the Japan Football League (JFL). Membership grew to about three thousand, and in 2000 attendance averaged about four thousand – far higher than any other JFL team, and more than many in J2. With Littbarski in charge, Yokohama walked away with the title the first two years. 'If we concentrate for ninety minutes, we can win every game 3– or 4–0,' Littbarski said at the time. 'But many times we go 1–0 up, and we get a little sad that the other team can't compete with us. So the players stop playing. Then we wake up and win 3–0. Competing – beating other people – is not what the Japanese like to do. If they win, they are embarrassed that the other team has lost.'

Based on these performances, from 2001 Yokohama FC played in the J.League, albeit J2, and the supporters had clambered back to the place they had been so rudely kicked out of. The club's annual revenues were only around 300 million yen (£1.7 million), roughly a third each from membership fees, gate receipts and sponsors. They struggled financially, and the team travelled between four different rented practice grounds. The supporters had failed to save the Flügels, or even obtain the right to use that name, but maybe they had gained something more important. 'Because of what's happened,' said Tamaki Kawamura, the Flügels supporter, who became part of the new club's management, 'we've realised as supporters that football isn't just entertainment that you turn up to. So there's a good side to all this.'

CHAPTER TWELVE

Go West

Hirokazu Shinotsuka was an average footballer at school, but that didn't stop him dreaming of international success. Entranced by the stories in *Captain Tsubasa* and *Eleven*, Japan's leading football comic books, whose heroes went to Brazil and became stars, at the age of sixteen he left for Brazil. There he bought a football education for about 80,000 yen (£500) a month, training at a series of clubs in the Sao Paulo and Minas Gerais state leagues. His parents gave him enough money to survive the first year. After that ran out he went back to Japan and worked on construction sites for six months to save money to spend more time in Brazil. 'I read these comics and I knew that Kazu had been to Brazil, and these made me want to go there,' he said later. 'There's an aspect of the Japanese that just likes things that look cool. For girls that means Gucci and Louis Vuitton products. For boys like me it was Brazilian football. And I thought it would enable me to play for Japan one day.'

When Kazu Miura went to Brazil in the 1980s, there were already a few dozen young Japanese training in Brazil. In the 1990s, the numbers swelled to the hundreds, and some Brazilian clubs had special dormitories for Japanese apprentices. Shinotsuka found out that top clubs such as Sao Paulo or Corinthians charged about 200,000 yen (£1,100) a month to Japanese youths wanting to train there, so he took the cut-price route. He lived in dormitories that sometimes had bunk beds, but often just mattresses on the floor. His staple diet was *feijoada* – a bean-based stew – and rice, a meal provided by the clubs, though usually not in large enough quantities. Occasionally, he treated himself and bought an egg and asked the kitchen to fry it. Other times a group of players put money together to buy a loaf of bread – communal bonding that wasn't reflected in the regular theft of his football kit by his fellow apprentices. Sometimes they helped themselves to his shampoo and toothpaste, too, but he soon got used to it. 'You can't do anything about that,' he said. 'It goes with the territory. They're not bad people – it's just how they are. At first I thought, "Hey! Why the hell are they taking my things?" But before long I started using theirs, too.'

After about four years, Shinotsuka's game had improved and he was enjoying life in Brazil despite its hardships. Travelling to away games, players brought along drums, and sang on the bus. They danced in the dressing room. 'In Japan they all listen to their own Walkmans, but in Brazil they sing together,' he said. 'At these times I felt, "Wow – I'm really in Brazil!"' He began to think he might make it as a professional, and even had offers from some small teams in country towns. But Brazilian regulations demanded that a foreign player make the equivalent of at least a few thousand dollars a month, and most of the several dozen Japanese footballers playing professionally there were in fact subsidising their own wages with money from Japan. 'Brazilians thought that Japanese players paid money to play,' said Shinotsuka. What's more, the team would have owned his 'pass' – a Brazilian system giving a club a form of ownership over a player's career. Joining a Brazilian club like this would have made it hard later to play in Japan and be selected for the national team. Aged twenty-one, he returned to Japan hoping to join a J.League club.

His timing could not have been worse. It was right after the Yokohama merger, and all J.League teams were cutting costs. What's more, Japanese clubs had become suspicious of players who had spent several years in Brazil, thinking that they had either been there just for fun, or because they had not been good enough to work their way through the Japanese system of high school and J.League youth teams. Around this time, the only top professional to emerge from a Brazilian odyssey was Yuji Nakazawa, the Verdy and Japan defender. Shinotsuka got no J.League tests. After about a year, he gave up and worked as an assistant chef in a French restaurant in Tokyo. He couldn't watch football on TV for a while because the very thought of the game overwhelmed him with feelings of failure. But he soon learned to bury himself in his new vocation, working six days a week, from 7.30 in the morning to midnight without a break. 'I want to go to France one day to study cooking properly,' he said. 'It's good to have a dream, though nothing is quite as good as football.'

Until the mid-1990s, Japan's ideas of sporting success mostly stretched no further than the shores of its archipelago. Interest in American baseball was limited to those former major-leaguers who came to play out their careers in Japan. And as the bubble economy was about to burst, the latest sporting craze was for sumo, as Takanohana, a nineteen-year-old wrestler and the scion of Japan's most powerful sumo dynasty, emerged to triumph over a handful of 200 kg-plus Hawaiian wrestlers. The Hawaiians had been challenging for supremacy in Japan's most traditional sport, and when this golden boy, who was a lithe 150–160 kg, trumped their bulk with his skill and nimbleness, Japan was delighted, as if it had been proved that the nation's artistry and technical prowess were in the end superior to the crude power of the West. With Japan rich beyond its wildest dreams, sport and much else happening outside the country might have a degree of interest – but ultimately didn't really matter. Even at the turn of the twenty-first century, the Japanese liked to contrast affairs in Japan with those in '*sekai*' – 'the world', as if they belonged to separate universes.

Japanese isolationism had origins going back to the Tokugawa Shogunate, which ruled Japan from 1600 to 1868, and feared that interference by foreigners and foreign ideas would threaten its rule. So it started a policy of national seclusion, and issued a series of five edicts between

1633 and 1639 that banned foreign travel (with a few minor exceptions, any Japanese caught trying to leave or return to Japan was to be executed) and forbade trade with the outside world (except with the Dutch and Chinese in the port of Nagasaki, and Koreans in Tsushima, another port). The Shogunate finally abandoned the policy after an American ship arrived in 1853 to demand diplomatic and commercial relations. Japan then began its campaign to absorb Western learning in order to catch up and overtake the West – a crusade that has continued almost to the present day.

The tradition of isolation and Japan's subsequent love-hate relationship with foreign culture created an intense interest for the Japanese in how they sized up against the West. Despite the country's status as the world's second biggest economic power, the Japanese still craved respect and approval from overseas, something that hit any foreigner who arrived in Japan and was asked for opinions of everything from the consumer electronics industry to cherry blossom. The desire for recognition eventually beat out the safer option of isolation, and by the mid-1990s, Japanese dreams of success had moved beyond their homeland.

Japan started to desire and celebrate international sporting success like a developing country does. Every Olympic medallist became a super-hero. Marathon runner Naoko Takahashi shot to fame after winning the Gold at Sydney, and became so popular she featured in TV ads for five companies in a single year, with products ranging from chewing gum to stock-broking. The first great breakthrough in team sports came in baseball, when pitcher Hideo Nomo joined the Los Angeles Dodgers in 1995 and was named the National League's Rookie of the Year. In 2001 there was even more excitement, this time when Ichiro Suzuki became Japan's first successful outfielder in the major leagues, picking up a hatful of batting records and the American League's Most Valuable Player title in his first year with the Seattle Mariners. Ichiro, as he liked to be known, was on TV far more than he ever had been when playing in Japan, when the relative obscurity of his team had kept him out of the limelight. With Ichiro and half a dozen other Japanese players active in the US, nightly news magazines on TV began to feature Major League news before that of Japan's own baseball leagues. Interest in domestic baseball dropped so dramatically that the sports papers were filled with speculation that Japan's baseball leagues might be forced into a programme of major reconstruction, with one or two teams merging or closing down.

Right from the start of the J.League, Japanese football had been more focused than other sports when it came to interaction with 'the world'. The first connection was achieved when overseas stars played in Japan. Next came international matches and the 1998 World Cup. But what the Japanese really wanted was to produce a genuine world-class player. In the *Captain Tsubasa* comic book, hero Tsubasa Ozora had for years been a school football star – which defined the dreams of most young Japanese until around 1990. But in the mid-1990s, his mission changed. He now had to lead Japan to victory in the World Cup, and so went off to learn 'world' football in Brazil, where he wore the number 10 shirt at Sao Paulo FC.

Despite the hundreds who tried, Japan's only real successes in overseas football until 1998 were Okudera, twenty years earlier, and Kazu during his time in Brazil. But even Kazu struggled at the highest level. A stint in the Serie A at Genoa in 1994/95 ended with a single goal and relegation for his team. He later played for Croatia Zagreb for several months in 1999, but was let go by Ossie Ardiles during his spell as manager there. But the new generation of Japanese footballers had grown up with professional football, foreign stars and World Cup hopes. For them, playing in Europe seemed less like a dream than a condition of adequacy.

When Hidetoshi Nakata had finished high school in 1995, almost all J.League clubs wanted to sign him. He told them he wanted to spend some time training overseas, and chose a club, Hiratsuka Bellmare, that promised to let him do this. As a result, he spent twenty days practising with the Juventus youth team, which was enough for him to decide he was as good as the top Italian players of his age. Three years later, after the 1998 World Cup, he was Japan's rising star. But by this time, more than just wanting to play abroad, he was desperate to leave Japan – in fact he felt he was running for his life. The cause lay in football's old, and so often inglorious, relationship with the media and a virulent form of nationalism that still survives in Japan. Football and nationalism are a natural couple, and this partnership brings with it trouble in every footballing nation. In Japan the problem was not national team supporters, who displayed nothing but hand-shaking, litter-clearing good manners, but a group of people who had nothing to do with football.

After Japan qualified for France, Nakata refused to talk to most news reporters. The tabloid press had already harassed and misquoted him enough in the past, and he thought the only way to stop them was silence. However, he trusted the respected broadsheet *Asahi Shimbun*, and agreed to be interviewed for one of a series of features on Japan's brightest hopes at the end of the century. One question the reporter asked him was why he didn't sing the national anthem, *Kimi ga yo*, before internationals. The tune's solemn chord changes give it a quiet dignity, inspiring the same sort of feelings in Japanese that church hymns do in the English, but it is not a stirring anthem of the kind to psyche up players before a football match. Though Nakata's reason for not singing was that, like a number of other players, he preferred to use the time to focus on the game ahead, he also told the reporter – but firmly off the record – about his feelings towards the anthem.

The feature appeared in January 1998, and played up Nakata's rising image as a nonconformist. 'There are lots of people who try to fit in with people around them,' he was quoted as saying, 'but I think they won't grow. People need to put across their own feelings more clearly. The Japanese national character has a part which likes to be taken along with the flow of things.' Finally, it was reported, he didn't sing along before games, because 'the national anthem is *dasai* – uncool or boring – and it makes people feel down.'

The Japanese media routinely avoided giving voice to criticism of national symbols like the imperial family. More than reverence, the main reason for this was fear of reprisals from Japan's small but violent band of ultra-nationalists, who wanted to revive the emperor-centred nationalism promoted before and during World War Two. A reporter on the liberal *Asahi* was shot dead by a rightist in 1987, while in 1993 another such extremist broke into that newspaper's offices, held senior editors hostage and eventually killed himself because he felt the paper had been making fun of rightists. The mayor of Nagasaki was shot and almost killed in 1990 for suggesting that Emperor Hirohito bore some responsibility for World War Two. Even if they were not actually violent, right-wingers routinely parked sound trucks outside the offices of companies they had a problem with, and blasted ear-splitting insults through loudspeakers. Another tactic was to harass programme sponsors and advertisers to get them to withdraw patronage from media that violated the nationalist code.

Such dogged people were not about to let Japan's latest hero get away with his apparent disrespect. They started with simple protests to the JFA, calling for Nakata to be dropped from the national team, and to Bellmare, demanding he hold a press conference to apologise. More nationalist groups joined in, and they started arriving at his management office in Tokyo. Then the demands were replaced by threats of violence. Soon Nakata was accompanied everywhere he went by a police patrol car, and after a while he moved into a hotel, which was easier to guard than his apartment, where he was attended round the clock by a personal bodyguard.

Nakata's agent, a woman called Etsuko Tsugihara, visited some of the groups to explain that his thinking was not actually as anti-establishment as the *Asahi* article had made it appear. But there were too many groups to deal with, and the threats continued. In April Nakata developed bad eczema over much of his body. By May, the eczema had spread to his face. The reasons for his condition were not known publicly at the time, and the press speculated that he was partying too much, or wasn't eating well (he was a committed carnivore, and didn't like vegetables). Doctors diagnosed stress, and Nakata missed a match against Paraguay in the Kirin Cup tournament, which was to serve as one of Japan's main warm-up games for the World Cup. He and Tsugihara spent in the region of 20 million yen (£100,000) on security and hotels over his three months of refuge, a cost that was not sustainable on his Bellmare salary. He even told her that it would be more sensible to give up football than die.

Fortunately, his performances before and during the World Cup had attracted attention from European clubs. Though he hadn't been the architect of any goals in France, his vision and passing ability convinced scouts that he could perhaps pass muster in Europe. The main interest came from Aston Villa and AC Perugia, a small Italian club that had just been promoted to Serie A. Perugia's owner invited him to a banquet at his castle, and presented him with a red Perugia shirt with his name and the number 8, his number in the Japan national team. The manager, Ilario Castagner, told him the newly promoted club was a candidate to go straight back down to Serie B, and that he wanted to rebuild the team round Nakata to ensure this didn't happen. At Aston Villa, manager John Gregory said he had read a scouting report describing Nakata as more talented than the young Dennis Law. But Gregory had not seen Nakata in action himself, and wanted him to travel to Birmingham to take part in training, or at least have someone from Aston Villa take a closer look at him play in Japan. But Nakata couldn't wait for Villa. He was nervous, isolated, and desperate to get out of Japan. In Japan, he told the writer of an authorised book, 'I have to be protected by someone, and I can't stand not being able to live from day to day. I am sick of living in fear.' Nakata opted for Perugia.

Perugia's first game of the 1998/99 Serie A season was against Juventus, then the Italian champions, who boasted some of the cream of the recent World Cup tournament, like Zinedine Zidane, Edgar Davids and Filippo Inzaghi. All Japan was watching and wanted to know: could Nakata cut it in this extraordinary company?

From his arrival in Perugia, the Japanese press followed his every move. Training sessions were surrounded by Japanese cameramen to the extent that Nakata's new teammates complained and demanded he control them. As well as the cameramen, the sports papers all stationed correspondents in Perugia. They had been ordered to file reports most days, but as Nakata refused to talk to them, they had very little material. So they wrote up Perugia's every practice game, and when they got desperate, the story became his bad relations with the Japanese press – as when a cameraman ran over to photograph him signing autographs for children, and Nakata told him: 'You're in the way! Go away, you worm!'

About 500 Japanese fans turned up to see how Nakata would fare against Juventus, and by halftime it looked like a disaster. Newly promoted Perugia were 3–0 down and looked hopelessly outclassed. But seven minutes into the second half, Nakata broke free near the goal line on the right, and fired a goal from a seemingly impossible angle. Another seven minutes later, the ball rebounded to him inside the Juventus penalty area after a corner. He half-volleyed, and sent the ball crashing into the back of the net. Then Nakata did something he didn't normally do: he clenched his fist and, just a little, punched the air in front of him. The final score was 4–3 to Juventus, and though Perugia had lost, they had not been disgraced.

Nakata blossomed in Italy. Though he had gone there known as an expert passer of the ball, he also soon developed into a fine dribbler and tenacious holder of the ball. He also scored ten goals in the 1998/99 season, and was the main reason that Perugia survived in Serie A that year. In 2000 he moved to AS Roma, and used some of his new wealth to help out his old club, Bellmare. Bellmare had been relegated to J2 and fallen into financial trouble. From 2000 Nakata sponsored the team, and they bore the logo of his website, nakata.net, on their shirts. At Roma, however, the rising Italian star Francesco Totti played in the same attacking midfield position as Nakata, and he got few starts. After playing a minor role in Roma's 2000/01 Scudetto triumph, Nakata transferred to Parma.

Nakata's success made him a hero to many young Japanese. His internet page averaged 700,000 hits a day, and described a life that had everything a young Japanese could want. In addition to his achievements on the field, he built up a large wardrobe of designer Italian clothes, ate out a lot, and gathered friends all over the world. His young Japanese fans admired him for this but were even more impressed by the very 'un-Japanese' way he approached life. Here was a man who had clearly broken free. When he received a stream of messages about his slump in form after moving to Parma, he explained how to approach such bumps in life's road: 'Regardless of what other people say, if you think you are right, you should do as you think best,' he wrote, before adding that 'the important thing is to have a strong sense of self.' This advice would cause endless trouble for any Japanese who followed it at work or in school. But Nakata had bucked the system and shown that even a Japanese could live by his own rules – most of the time, that is. At Japan internationals around 2000, he started moving his lips, but not quite singing, to the national anthem.

Not only had Nakata helped Perugia avoid relegation, he had also made them piles of money from replica shirt sales in Japan and his transfer fee to Roma. So as well as proving to other Japanese footballers that making it overseas was a possibility, he also convinced European clubs that they might be worth trying out as an untapped source of talent. The first few struggled. Jubilo Iwata midfielder Hiroshi Nanami spent a lot of time on the Venezia bench in the 1999/2000 season, because his cultured left foot was not matched by an ability to handle rough play. He returned to Japan after the club was relegated to Serie B, but seemed toughened by the experience. Shoji Jo scored two goals for Real Valladolid in Spain, and then went back to Yokohama F Marinos, where he lost his form and was no longer picked for the national team. Akinori Nishizawa flopped during several months at Espanyol, and though he got a second chance in Europe with Bolton Wanderers, he returned to Japan without featuring in any Premier League games.

A group of younger players looked more promising, however. During the 1990s, the JFA built up a 'Training Centre' system – not a network of physical centres, but a nationwide coaching and scouting scheme modelled loosely on that in France. This ran seminars, and issued guidelines for coaches at schools and clubs around the country. It also spotted talented youngsters and brought them to elite training camps several times a year, where they could practise under top coaches along with the best players of their age. Another boost came from the youth teams attached to J.League clubs, which provided an alternative to high school football. As a result of this progress, Japan's under-twenty team were runners-up in the 1999 World Youth Championship. In 2001, Junichi Inamoto moved to Arsenal from Gamba Osaka; Urawa Reds midfielder Shinji Ono, probably the most talented Japanese player of this generation, went to Feyenoord; and Naohiro Takahara moved from Jubilo to Boca Juniors in Argentina.

Explaining their moves overseas, the young players universally cited lofty ideals, and said they were going for self-enhancement and to prove that they were good enough for the world outside Japan. 'I want to improve myself,' said Inamoto of his move to Arsenal in 2001, using a word that literally meant he wanted to 'polish' himself. Naohiro Takahara said exactly the same thing of his move to Boca

Juniors. 'I think Italy has things that are lacking in myself,' Nanami had said when he signed for Venezia. 'I want to find these.' And that seemed to be enough to convince the Japanese public. No matter that they had chucked in their Japanese clubs because they thought they could do better for themselves by leaving for overseas. If this process improved them, and they could serve their nation that much better in 2002; and if they could raise the highly sensitive national self-esteem by making it big overseas, then that made up for everything.

Each one of these brave young lads set off into the great wide world to a never-diminishing hoopla. At bizarre sayonara ceremonies after their last games in Japan, they gave speeches thanking fans for their support and promising to do their best abroad, often to tear-jerking background music. In Inamoto's case he was sent off to the strains of 'Imagine', as crying female fans shrieked 'Inaah!' and held up banners saying, 'Do your best at Arsenal!' Some of these festivals doubled normal match attendance and transcended club loyalties. Once the players arrived at their destinations, their progress, or lack of it, was covered in laborious detail by the Japanese media. When Yoshikatsu Kawaguchi moved to Portsmouth, the sports papers started carrying regular reports of Pompey's matches in the Nationwide League. When a player didn't make the first team, like Inamoto at Arsenal and Nishizawa at Bolton, the papers ran reports of their reserve-team games. Football tourism began to focus on the European teams Japanese players had joined. 'It gives people a purpose for travelling abroad,' explained Toru Rokugawa, editor in chief of *Calcio 2002*, a magazine that focused on Italian football. 'Everyone has now been to Guam and Hawaii, so it's more fun to go somewhere and support Japan. It's a way to express national pride.'

One of the more bizarre examples of Japan's hunger for overseas success came after the virtually unknown Nozomi Hiroyama persuaded his club JEF United to rent him out to Cerro Porteño in Paraguay in 2001. There, Hiroyama started making appearances in the Copa Libertadores and became the first Japanese to participate in that prestigious South American club cup competition. TV news and sports programmes began to show highlights of his games, and newspapers printed regular dispatches from Paraguay, a country that rarely blipped on Japan's national radar, about the latest match played by a football team almost no Japanese had ever heard of. Previously ignored in Japan, Hiroyama was selected as a substitute for the national team in the 2001 Kirin Cup, and suddenly found the whole nation rooting for him. The crowd and TV commentators became desperate for the manager to bring him on, chanting his name or speculating excitedly about his forthcoming appearance. (He stayed on the bench.)

While the best struggled to survive in Europe, even those Japanese players who stayed at home found there was no longer any refuge from the rigours of the world game. The 1998 World Cup and its qualifying process had shown that Japan were now a top team in Asia, but could not yet compete with the best countries in the world. To remedy this, the JFA once again looked abroad for a national team manager. Arsène Wenger was the perennial first choice for the job, but since he was engaged elsewhere, they took on a coach recommended by Wenger, Philippe Troussier. Frenchman Troussier had spent a decade in Africa, and towards the end coached Nigeria during their successful qualification campaign for the 1998 World Cup, and then South Africa during the finals. In Africa he had earned the nickname 'White Witchdoctor'. In Japan, the press called him 'Red Devil' due to the colour his face turned when he was angry.

Advice to foreigners going to work in Japan usually includes: sort out any problems quietly and in private; do not cause colleagues to lose face in front of others; never lose your temper. In other words maintain *wa* – harmony – Japan's national virtue. But Troussier did things his way. He publicly accused the JFA, his employers, of operating like 'amateurs'. He complained that the J.League was so easygoing that Japanese players had no fight in them. He balled out individual players in front of the team. In April 2000, after a string of disappointing results, including draws against China and South Korea, Japanese newspapers reported that the JFA had decided to fire him.

When he first arrived in Japan, had Troussier decided, 'The younger Japanese players are maybe better than Europeans in technical areas. My challenge is to prepare the players for world football – to play against aggressive foreign sides.' In inimitable style, he set about bringing them up to international norms. Some of his training sessions looked like rugby, as he pushed and shoved his young charges round the field. Away from the football field he was a warm, friendly man. But his dressing room tirades often seem designed to intimidate players, provoking one to announce to his face: 'I don't like you.' After a jet-lagged Japan were beaten 5–0 by France in a Paris friendly, Troussier decided the players needed toughening up even more. 'We are not playing Thailand or Vietnam,' he told them. 'If you keep playing like this we will never be able to compete against the best in the world. You are not girls.' He made them do one exercise that involved a player pushing the ball between two defenders standing close together, and then barging through the middle. During this drill, Ryuzo Morioka, one of Asia's top defenders, aggravated an ankle injury and fell down clutching it in pain. 'Get out! We don't need you!' was Troussier's furious response.

Despite the widely held idea that diplomacy works best in Japan, Troussier's abrasive style appeared to kindle the sort of competitive spirit the Japanese needed. The 2000 Olympic team won all seventeen of its matches in the run-up to Sydney, notching up an overall scoring record of 84–5, and provoking chants in the stands of 'Troussier Nippon!' In the dressing room the players began to sing to celebrate victories. They had watched a documentary broadcast on Japanese television about France's 1998 World Cup campaign, and seen that after games they won, the French team chanted a slowed-down version of the orchestral interlude in 'I Will Survive'. The Japan Olympic team were impressed by this, and started doing the same after their victories. Troussier used Japanese interpreters for dealings with the JFA and the domestic press, but talked to the players through a young French linguist who spoke – or shouted – in the same tone as Troussier to ensure the message was not diluted. 'I need my culture,' he explained. 'It is very important for me to have a French interpreter.'

After two years, Troussier was given a new two-year contract with a 25 per cent pay rise (to an annual 100 million yen – £560,000). Japan lost to the USA on a penalty shootout in Sydney's knockout stage, but shortly afterwards became Asian champions for the second time. In 2001 they reached the final of the eight-team Confederations Cup, losing to France by just a single goal. Explaining his confrontational management style, Troussier said: 'It would be impossible for a Japanese coach to act like me. A Japanese must respect social conventions. But I have not been influenced by things in Japan, and it's a great advantage. You need human talent on a football field – to communicate and make decisions under pressure. Japanese players need to walk around London or eat pizza in Italy, because this will break down the social borders and give them new ways to express themselves. They do not know enough about the world, so it is important for them to have human experiences.'

EPILOGUE

The 2002 World Cup was Japan's opportunity to show off. The hardware was in place – ten gleaming stadiums, all built at great expense in the previous five years. The question was how Japan would cope with the World Cup's human side, the football and the festivals.

Losing all three games in France had been forgivable: Japan had been playing away from home in their first ever World Cup, and qualification was an achievement in itself. This time was different. They qualified automatically as co-hosts, and expectations were higher. The squad was much more experienced, having played as professionals in the J.League from the beginning of their careers, and several had played professionally overseas. This time too, the JFA had hired a foreign manager, Philippe Troussier, especially to prepare for the event. They also had home advantage in the form of crowds and were accustomed to the humidity of the rainy season, when the weather varied from warm and muggy to hot and steamy, and the moist air clung to its heat in the evenings. Failing to win a game – let alone lose all three again – would bring terrible humiliation.

Off the field, the World Cup provided a showcase for a country that had moved on from the stereotypes of its economic superpower era. J.League founder Saburo Kawabuchi had intended that football should help change Japan, and while much of the country remained untouched by the game's influence, football had been one of the positive aspects of a decade of economic decline. The world no longer saw Japan as a land of geisha, sumo and dark-suited *salarymen*. Instead, Japan was increasingly known as a land of bottle-blonde women, video games and the world's most fashionably dressed youth.

These shifts did not guarantee that Japan was ready for the arrival of hundreds of thousands of foreigners – and football fans, no less. Japan had already hosted three Olympic Games, two winter and one summer. But while these brought large numbers of athletes and officials to the country, the rest of the world watched on TV. Football came accompanied by a whole culture of fandom, plus armies of supporters. The game thrived on noise and tension, and both celebrations and expressions of regret often spilled out on to the streets. Sometimes it was hard to tell when a crowd was having innocent fun or when it was potentially dangerous. Other recent World Cup hosts, like Italy, the USA and France, had big holiday industries, and were used to hoards of people arriving to hang out. Japan had spent hundreds of years either shutting itself away from the outside world or competing against it. It attracted far fewer tourists, and many of those that did come were the posh type who visited temples in Kyoto. People looking for bars and fun were a rarity. Moreover, while Tokyo's population was relatively wealthy and urban, long used to exotic holidays and seeing foreigners in the street, no matches were scheduled for the capital. Outside the biggest cities, foreigners could still find themselves stared at like alien beings or turned away from *pensions*.

At first, many Japanese closest to the action appeared to wish the World Cup would go away. Of course, sweet-faced children and women in kimonos showed the genteel face of the country as they turned out to welcome teams to their camps. And the new generation of international football fanatics scrambled for tickets to catch a live glimpse of Gabriel Batistuta, Allessandro Del Piero or Michael Owen. But shopkeepers in Osaka and Yokohama took out riot insurance, and even law enforcement seemed nervous. Japanese police hadn't dealt with a riot since the student demonstrations of the 1960s, and most cities had never experienced one. In addition to water cannon and shields, they tried out new gadgets, including a Spiderman-type gun that fired a net round culprits. They underwent special training sessions in which officers and actors dressed up as hooligans in Union Jack T-shirts. The TV networks eagerly broadcast these mock riots, planting the idea in the public mind that this was the kind of action they should expect.

In Sapporo, courts adjusted their schedules to deal with an expected rash of prosecutions around the England vs. Argentina game. The city even booked a car transporter to ship the hundreds of anticipated hooligans to a detention centre near Tokyo. In Niigata, where a shortage of accommodation was already seen as a major problem, a group of hoteliers decided to close for the duration of the World Cup because they didn't want foreigners staying. Elderly farmers with land near the stadium made it clear that they had no interest in football and had never wanted the World Cup. One old lady showed a TV interviewer how her storm shutters and pet dog would keep the hooligans out, while a pub owner brandished the baseball bat that he intended to repel aggressors with. More than the world's greatest sporting festival, much of Japan appeared to be expecting an enemy invasion.

No one seemed very excited about the football. The 1964 Olympics had represented Japan's recovery from the rubble of World War II. The capital boasted a new network of overhead motorways, and the first bullet trains ran just weeks before the start of the games. People remembered the Tokyo Olympics over thirty years later as the defining event of Japan's post-war development. For the World Cup, no matches in Tokyo meant it was hard to make the tournament into a national focus point. Moreover, there wasn't even an opening ceremony to build up to – that was taking place in South Korea because of the strange co-hosting arrangement FIFA had dreamt up. So on the day of the opening ceremony in Seoul, the World Cup felt simply like something happening in another country.

Then, after Ireland played Cameroon in the first Japanese match in Niigata, the *Asahi* newspaper's headline declared: '*Sekai ga kita*' ('The world has arrived'). And, despite the fears, 'the world' turned out to be fun.

As one section of the population fretted about hooligans, another began to develop different expectations of what the World Cup would bring. When the teams began to arrive at training camps in obscure towns and villages around the country, they were mobbed. Crowds of women turned out to drool over and wave at the Italian team, who were dubbed the 'Band of Handsome Men'. Daytime TV shows compiled charts of the best-looking players in the competition: Italian captain Francesco Totti was popular, but the undisputed winner was David Beckham.

Beckham had taken up a bizarre, 'soft-Mohawk' style – the result you'd expect if a latter-day punk mated with Sonic the Hedgehog. By the time the World Cup kicked off this was the coolest haircut in Japan. The better hairdressers had soon mastered the technique and offered 'Beckham Cuts' to Japanese fashion clones. His clothes too defined the look for the summer: a combination of the haircut, a wispy beard, football shirt, sunglasses and baggy shorts. After the World Cup, Beckham became a star in Japanese advertising. He and wife Victoria were photographed lounging in each other's arms in front of a fire, their regular features hinting at the results that cosmetics and facial treatments from TBC (Tokyo Beauty Centre) could produce. In his Manchester United shirt, he became the poster boy for Vodafone's Japanese affiliate, J-Phone. Meiji Seika, one of Japan's biggest confectioners, erected a three-metre chocolate statue of him in Shibuya, young Tokyo's favourite hang-out.

So Japan decided to the enjoy the World Cup, much like it had decided to enjoy football in the first place – not taking it as seriously as football's Old World, but making up the difference with innocent fun. Japan games were sold out and avidly watched on television – the game against Russia in Yokohama attracted the second highest audience ever for a sporting event. Crowds of 50,000 turned out to watch the home team's games on a giant screen in Tokyo's

National Stadium, where they could enjoy a big-crowd atmosphere even without the football. But what really stood out was how the Japanese adopted other countries' national teams. Young Japanese flooded Roppongi, Tokyo's traditional foreigner haunt, to hang out with visiting fans – and wear their team shirts. England's white strip was the most popular, with Beckham's number seven inevitably leading the way. Other front-runners were the Ireland, Brazil and Italy strips. Instead of violent drunks rampaging and attacking the local populace, genial drunks made friends with the locals on Roppongi's streets, where they chanted or delivered a few choruses of a supporters' song before moving on to the next bar.

Trouble just wasn't on the agenda. British police had confiscated the passports of hundreds of known hooligans, and helped Japanese immigration identify and turn away fifty-three who actually made it to Japan. Ahead of England's match against Sweden in Saitama, local shops formed a vigilance committee to patrol the streets and protect children from hooligans. In the end, all that happened outside Saitama Stadium 2002 was that England fans drank beer with young Japanese who had donned the white shirt to become England supporters for a few weeks. There were a total of ninety-three arrests in Japan during the World Cup, and the main crime was ticket touting. Only thirteen Britons were nabbed, all for minor infringements that never made the news. The nationality that got into the most trouble, with sixty arrests, was Japanese – and one of the biggest causes was over-celebration.

Despite the progress made by the national team, their warm-up games were miserable and for the same reason as always: inability to score goals. They strung together lots of nice passes in midfield, but didn't seem to know what do after that. On a trip to Europe, they lost 1–0 to Real Madrid and then 3–0 to Norway. In home-practice matches, they beat Slovakia 1–0, but only managed draws with Honduras, Costa Rica and Sweden, with the goals coming from midfield instead of the strikers. Japan's first World Cup game, against Belgium in Saitama, looked like it might go the same way. The first half ended in deadlock, and twelve minutes into the second Belgium's veteran captain Marc Wilmots leant back and fired a beautiful overhead kick past Japanese goalkeeper Seigo Narazaki.

But that setback was the cue for Japanese football to show it had progressed. The Japan team was among the youngest in the World Cup, with most players under twenty-five. Many had come up through the new national training programme instituted when the J.League started. As if to emphasise their youth and difference, all but one player in the starting line-up against Belgium had dyed their hair, the shades ranging from moderate chestnut browns all the way to Junichi Inamoto's silver rinse. The only exception was Shinji Ono, the Feyenoord midfielder, who had shaved all his hair off. Instead of acknowledging their inferiority and drooping like they had when a goal down in the past, the Japanese concentrated harder and picked up the pace of the game. Two minutes after they went behind, a long pass bounced ahead of Takayuki Suzuki as he hurtled forward pursued by a Belgium defender. The ball was just too far in front of Suzuki, but he was determined. Still at full speed, he stretched out his foot and poked the ball past the Belgium goalkeeper. Japan had scored – and scored from a half-chance. Next came Inamoto's turn to impress his doubters. He had just spent a year at Arsenal where he did not once play in the Premier League, and made just a handful of appearances from the bench in Champions League and Worthington Cup ties. But the training sessions and rest seemed to have improved him, and he suddenly hit form. Eight minutes after Suzuki's goal, he began a smart run from midfield and followed this with a pinpoint shot that put Japan in the lead. He later had a goal disallowed on a technicality. Fifteen minutes from time the Belgians equalised, but Japan had gained their first ever World Cup point.

Six days later it got even better. Japan played Russia, and a scrappy hard-fought first half produced no shots on target.

But six minutes into the second, Japan strung together a world-class move. Koji Nakata drove the ball forward to Atsushi Yanagisawa on the edge of the Russian penalty area. He flicked it through to Inamoto on the edge of the goal area, and the striker scored again, high into the roof of the Russian net. That was enough for Japan's first World Cup victory, by one goal to nil.

After the final whistle, Japan celebrated like never before. Prime Minister Junichiro Koizumi, who had just seen his first football match, congratulated the players in the dressing room, grinning and brandishing a blue plastic loud hailer. The players responded with a '*Koi-zu-mi!*' chant. Throughout the rest of Japan, young people went nuts. In Osaka, several hundred jumped off a bridge into the Dotombori River, the polluted waterway running through the city's entertainment district. In Tokyo, cars sounded their horns and waved Japanese flags in the streets of Shibuya. A crowd gathered in the central pedestrian precinct and jumped up and down, chanting players' names and '*Troussier Nippon!*' The police looked grumpy but mostly stayed quiet, just dragging down a few young men who scaled the roof of an underground railway entrance. They made a few arrests in each major city, but these were for high jinks rather than violence: some were for indecent exposure as men stripped for joy, while the rest were for 'obstructing police duties' – in other words, objecting to being ordered around by officers who turned out in unnecessary numbers. But most fans brushed off the police presence. In Shibuya, they danced and sang for hours, and then at around 2 a.m. stopped their usual chants and switched – in a mixture of tribute, sympathy and sarcasm – to: '*Keisatsu saiko!*' – ('The police are great!'). Five days later Japan beat Tunisia 2–0, again through opportunistic goals. Substitute Hiroaki Morishima scored early in the second half with his first touch of the ball, and Nakata netted with a rare header. The celebrations erupted all over again.

Japan's World Cup came to an end on a miserable, rainy day in Miyagi, a prefecture north-east of Tokyo which had built a stadium with a track in some far-off hills. Troussier had been an effective manager because he had always chosen younger players, and insisted that they roughen up their game so they could mix it with more aggressive teams. Despite an abrasive style, his results had gained him a basic level of respect in Japan, if not much affection. But for Japan's game against Turkey in the knockout stage, Troussier made an elementary coaching error: he changed a winning team. Out went the two regular strikers, Suzuki – a physical target man who had scored Japan's first goal of the tournament – and the quick, creative Yanagisawa. In their place came two surprises. One was Akinori Nishizawa, who had previously spent several months at Bolton Wanderers without actually playing in the Premier League, and was now short of match practice after recovering from an operation. The other was Alex, a fast, skilful Brazilian who had taken Japanese nationality, but normally played on the left of midfield or as a wing back. After Turkey scored from a corner thirteen minutes into the game, Japan couldn't pull level. By the closing stages they knew they were not going to score and played that way. Japan lost 1–0.

Still, Japan's success was one of a number of results in 2002 that indicated the game might be going through a major power shift. The two pre-tournament favourites, Argentina and champions France, came from football's Old World – and they limped out in the group stage. Though the eventual finalists were traditional old powers – Brazil and Germany – joining them in the semi-finals were Turkey, in their first World Cup appearance since 1958, and South Korea. Despite five previous appearances, Japan's co-hosts had never previously won a World Cup match. This time, with Dutch coaching, spirited running and some helpful refereeing decisions, they claimed two of the biggest scalps in the game, Italy and Spain.

A new pattern in the game was emerging, with players from all over Africa and, more recently, Asia assembled at top European clubs. There they honed skills that would eventually benefit their countries in international competition. The Japanese were no exception, and by early 2003 half a dozen of their players were on the books of clubs in Europe's top leagues. Midfielder Shunsuke Nakamura, overlooked by Troussier for the World Cup, followed Nakata to Italy, where he played for Reggina in the Serie A. Striker Naohiro Takahara, who had missed the tournament through illness, joined Hamburger SV in Germany. Takayuki Suzuki played for Belgian champions KRC Genk. And Inamoto finally got to play in the Premier League – not for Arsenal, but at Fulham. He also scored a hat trick in the Intertoto Cup final against Bologna, putting the club into the UEFA Cup for the first time in its history. Kazuyuki Toda signed for Tottenham Hotspur.

Kawabuchi said later he had shed tears after the victory over Russia in the World Cup. At the end of the tournament, he resigned as J.League chairman to head the JFA. His first decision was to appoint Zico to succeed Troussier as the Japan manager who would harness the new generation of talent. Kawabuchi could take credit for laying the groundwork for the success. Many countries had gone from obscurity to a good World Cup run in the past, but nowhere could boast the speed of Japan's overall football development, from local clubs to the national team. Pre-J.League, there had been no more than a few dozen grass pitches in the whole of Japan. To spur the creation of more, the JFA had made it a condition for candidates hosting World Cup team camps that they have at least two grass football pitches, and applications had come from eighty locations. In total, Kawabuchi guessed there were now more than five hundred grass pitches in Japan. Football also continued its mission to bring life and pride to sleepy provincial cities. After Vegalta Sendai were promoted from J2 to the top flight in 2002, they went on a winning streak and regularly packed out their 20,000-seat stadium. Three months after the World Cup, on 25 September, 39,000 people turned up to Niigata Stadium to see a second-division game on a weekday evening. 'In the past ten years a miracle has occurred,' Kawabuchi said.

As JFA president, Kawabuchi renamed his post 'Captain' to give a greater sense of on-the-ground leadership. He also decided to pay himself – not just for the sake of his wallet, but to move the JFA away from its amateur traditions towards a professional organisation. He then continued to make plans with the confidence that Japanese football was new enough to choose its own future. To raise the level of the game in Japan, for example, he set up 'J Academy' – a football programme for pre-school children. The period from age eight to twelve was the golden age for player development, Kawabuchi argued. To make the most of this time, the J Academy would nurture coordination and sense of balance from an early age. 'If we don't start this kind of programme, we will not reach the top in the world,' he insisted. 'I think it would be good if over the next decade Japan became the kind of country that regularly finished in the best ten at the World Cup.'

ACKNOWLEDGEMENTS

This book was only possible because of the generosity and cooperation of many people connected with Japanese football, including officials, coaches, players and fans. All the interviewees listed below gave me their time and knowledge with the openness and enthusiasm that characterises the Japanese football world. In cases where subjects were unavailable for interview I relied on written sources, which are listed separately.

   In addition, I am grateful to several friends for their help and encouragement while I was struggling with this project. I am particularly indebted to Robert Whiting and Velisarios Kattoulas for the vast amounts of feedback and advice they provided. Thanks to Jeff Kingston for tips on Japanese history, Paul Eckert for help on Korea and Shinichiro Tanaka for digging out obscure newspaper and magazine articles. Rachel Cugnoni at Yellow Jersey made invaluable suggestions for improvement, and copyeditor Matthew Parker smoothed out many wrinkles later on. Thanks also to my agent, John Pawsey, for finding Yellow Jersey in the first place.

Interviews:

Ossie Ardiles, Stuart Baxter, Dettmar Cramer, Gert Engels, Don Goodman, Takeo Goto, Kunishige Kamamoto, Hisayuki Kanda, Hideki Kato, Saburo Kawabuchi, Yoshikatsu Kawaguchi, Tamaki Kawamura, Toru Kawazu, Eijun Kiyokumo, Narumi Komatsu, Hisashi Komoto, Sadao Konuma, Yoichi Kozuma, Gary Lineker, Pierre Littbarski, Wagner Lopes, Koji Maeda, Kazuyoshi Miyazaki, Ignace

Mofeka, Leslie Mottram, Tetsuo Nakanishi, Tadakatsu Nishi, Kenji Ohba, Takeshi Okada, Yasuhiko Okudera, Hans Ooft, Tsunayoshi Ota, Michael Pao, Steve Perryman, Carlos Queiroz, Toru Rokugawa, Kazuki Sasaki, Hiroshi Sato, Hirokazu Shinotsuka, Yoshinori Shiwa, Dragan Stojkovic, Yasuo Suzuki, Masayuki Tamaki, Philippe Troussier, Tomio Tsujino, Asahi Ueda, Kazuo Uegaki, Frans van Balkom, Robert Whiting, Masatoshi Yamada, Mario Yamaguchi, Yoichi Yamamoto, Yoshiharu Yamamoto, Takayoshi Yamano, Jorge Yonashiro, Masatoshi Yoshida, Koichi Yoshizawa, Yoshimitsu Yui.

BIBLIOGRAPHY

Akutsu, Kenji: *Careca*, Sanichi Shobo, 1997

Asahi Shimbun: *J.League wa Kankyakusu Mizumashi Shima-sen*, Asahi Shimbun, 27 December 1992

Awata, Fusaho: *J.League kaze – Cho-shohishakai no Keizai-gaku*, Wedge, 1994

Ayano, Masaru: *Kazu Jugo no Tabidachi – Miura Kazuyoshi Monogatari*, Shogakkan, 1997

Bartholet, Jeffrey: *That's Godzillla at Bat*, Newsweek, 15 July 1996

Baxter, Stuart: *Katsu tame no Soshikiryoku – Nihon Soccer ga Kagayaku Shunkan*, Kodansha, 1996

Bungeishunju (ed.), *Nakata Goroku*, Bungeishunju, 1998

Campbell, Joseph: *The Hero With A Thousand Faces*, Bollingen Foundation / Princeton University Press, 1949

Crazy Calls and Todoroki, Yukio: *The Red Book*, Daiei Shuppan, 1994

Dunga (Carlos Caetano Bledorn Verri): *Seleção*, NHK Shuppan, 1998

—: *Nihon Senshu wa World Cup Shutsujo ga ikani Nihonkoku ni totte Juyo ka o Rikai Shite-inai!* (interview), Sapio, 4 February 1998

Etsugo, Sergio: *J.League Dai-14 Setsu Yokohama F – C Osaka / Chanto Soccer Shinasai* (column), Nikkan Sports, 1 November 1999

Goto, Takeo: *Topics from Within – Farewell Arsène Wenger*, Sports Graphic Number, 10 October 1996

Gunji, Sadanori: *Ooft kakumei – Katsu tame no Jinzai to Soshiki o do Tsukuru ka*, Shodensha, 1993

Ihara, Masami: *NO.1 Libero e no Michi (The Way of No.1 Libero)*, Tokyo FM Shuppan, 1995

Ishii, Shuichi (ed.): *1998-nendo J.League Pro Soccer Players Meikan*, Nikkan Sports Shuppansha, 1998

Isshi, Haruo: *Tatta Hitori no World Cup – Miura Kazuyoshi, 1,700 Hi no Tatakai*, Gentosha, 1998

J.League Yearbook 2001 Editorial Committee (ed.): *J.League Yearbook 2001*, J.League Enterprises, 2001

J.League Internet home page (http://www.j-league.or.jp/index.html)

Jo, Shoji: *Ace no Jo*, Riyon-sha, 1998

Kamamoto, Kunishige: *Sakka ni Moeta Hibi*, Jitsugyo no Nihonsha, 1985

—: *Goal no Kiseki*, Baseball Magazine-sha, 1995

Kamo, Shu: *Modern Soccer e no Chosen*, Kodansha, 1997

Kaneko, Tastsuhito: *28-nenme no Halftime*, Bungeishunju, 1997

—: *Kessen Zenya*, Shinchosha, 1998

Kato, Eiji: *Sakka to Taiki Shita Otoko Shigeo Yaegashi*, Sanichi Shobo, 1998

Kato, Kosho: *Kazu The Superstriker*, Footwork Publishing Corp., 1993

Kawabata, Yasuo: *Masayuki Okano The Greatest Hunter Rush to Goal!!*, Young Sunday, 5 February 1998

Kimura, Yukihiko: *Hokori – Dragan Stojkovic no Kiseki*, Tokyo Shimbun Shuppan-kyoku, 1998

Kodansha Ltd.: *Encyclopedia of Japan*, 1999

Komatsu, Narumi: *Nakata Hidetoshi Godo*, Gentosha, 1999

Konuma, Sadao: *Soccer de Manabe! Omae-tachi*, Kodansha, 1983

Korean Football Association Internet home page (http://www11.kfa.or.kr/football/home)

Lopes, Wagner: *Lopes*, Shogakkan, 1998

Masujima, Midori: *Kawabuchi Saburo – J.League, Kozoteki Kekkan ni yoru Kiki*, Sports Graphic Number, 31 December 1998

McNeill, David: *Media Intimidation in Japan: A Close Encounter with Hard Japanese Nationalism*, Electronic Journal of Contemporary Japanese Studies (www.japanesestudies.org.uk), 27 March 2001

Moffett, Sebastian: *Soccer Salvation*, Far Eastern Economic Review, 28 May 1998

—: Japan's Soccer Teams Struggle to Connect With Potential Fans, International Herald Tribune, 26 April 1999

—: *In Japan, It's Sayonara for Corporate-Sponsored Sports Teams*, International Herald Tribune, 11 November 1999

—: *French Coaching Style Stirs Japanese*, International Herald Tribune, 14 September 2000

—: *As Fans Build a Team of Their Own . . . . Yokohama Readies for the World Cup*, Business Week (International), 11 December 2000

—: Japanese Soccer Loses a Burning Star, International Herald Tribune, 1 June 2001

Moffett, Sebastian and Lee, Charles S.: *Political Football: Old Wounds are Reopened as Japan and South Korea Battle for the 2002 World Cup*, Far Eastern Economic Review, 23 May 1996

Motokawa, Etsuko: *U-22 Philippe Troussier to Platinum Age no 419 Nichi*, Shogakkan, 2000

Naganuma, Ken: *Kura-san no 'Soccer Goroku'*, Bungeishunju, 1970 (1)

Nakata, Hidetoshi (ed.): *Akka!! Hide to Nakata Zenkiroku*, Shinchosha, 1998

—: *'First of all, one win!'*, Hide's Mail, Hidetoshi Nakata Official Homepage (www.nakata.net), 22 September 2001

Nihon Soccer Kyokai – Gijutsu I-inkai: *Kyoka Shidoshin 2000-nenban*, Zaidan-hojin Nihon Soccer Kyokai, 2000

Nihon Soccer Kyokai Henshu I-inkai: *The Japan Football Association (JFA) 75-nen-shi*, Zaidan-hojin Nihon Soccer Kyokai, 1996

Ohsumi, Yoshiyuki: *Urawa Reds no Kofuku*, Aspect, 1998

Ohsumi, Yoshiyuki (ed.): *21-seiki no Sports ni Mukete*, Nihon Pro Soccer League, 2001

Oka, Kuniyuki: *Kazu to J.League*, Sanichi Shobo, 1993

—: *Kami-sama Zico no Message*, Sanichi Shobo, 1994

Ooft, Hans: *Nihon Soccer no Chosen (The Challenge of Japanese Soccer)*, Kodansha, 1993

Oshima, Hiroshi: *Nikkan kick-off densetsu*, Jitsugyo no Nihonsha, 1996

Parkinson, Lesley and Matsuda, Hiro: *Lineker – Ai Suru J.League e no Chokugen*, Kodansha, 1994

Publicity Institute Inc.: *Yasuhiko Okudera Professional Road*, Nihon Bunka Shuppan, 1987

Saeki, Toshio: *21-seiki ni okeru Kigyo Sports no Arikata*, Kigyo Sports Summit Ronbunshu (Osaki Kigyo Sports Jigyo Kenkyu Josei Zaidan), 19 January 1999

Sankei Sports: *Lineker Intai*, Sankei Sports, 22 September 1994

Shiwa, Yoshinori: *Katsu tame ni Nani o Shita ka*, Nikkan Sports Shuppansha, 1999

Suzuki, Takeshi: *Tennohai 65-nenshi*, Zaidan-hojin Nihon Sakka Kyokai (JFA), 1987

Takahashi, Yoichi: *Captain Tsubasa (World Youth-hen) – Kami no ko Santana no kan*, Shueisha, 1995

Takeuchi, Hiroshi: *2002-nen no Fair Play*, Kyodo Tsushinsha, 1996

Tamaki, Masayuki: *J.League Kara no Kaze*, Shueisha, 1993

Tamura, Shuichi: *The Face of Arsene Wenger*, Sports Graphic Number, March 1996

Tanaka, Koichi: *Shimizu S-Pulse – Aratanaru Chosen*, Tokyo FM Shuppan, 1998

Troussier, Philippe and Tamura, Shuichi: *Troussier Kakumei*, Shinchosha, 2001

Tsujino, Tomio: *Bokura ga Okoshita F no Kiseki*, Shogakkan, 1999

Ubukata, Yukio: *J.League no Keizaigaku*, Asahi Shimbunsha, 1994

Ueda, Asahi: *Nekkyo Road*, Za Masada, 1998

Urawa Red Diamonds: *Urawa Reds Official Handbook 1997*, Asutoro, Shuppan, 1997

Watanabe, Saburo: *F no Higeki*, Bunkasha, 1999

Wenger, Arsène: *Shosha no Esprit*, NHK Shuppan, 1997

Whiting, Robert: *The Chrysanthemum And The Bat*, Dodd, Mead & Co., 1977

—: *You Gotta Have Wa*, Vintage Books, 1989

Yamaguchi, Motohiro: *Yokohama Flügels – Shometsu no Kiseki*, Nihon Bungeisha, 1999

Yamaoka, Junichiro: *Reds to Urawa – Jun-ai Soccer Monogatari*, Ronsosha, 1998

Yamazaki, Koichi: *World Cup wa Nihonjin ga 'Nationalism' o Sotaika Shi*, Gakushu Suru Kakko no Kyozai da, Sapio, 4 February 1998

Yoshizawa, Koichi (ed.): *Bokutachi no World Cup – Supporter ga Mita! France e no Atsuki Kiseki*, Kobunsha, 1998

Zico: *Zico no Leader-ron*, Goma Shobo, 1993

—: *Zico no 'Shori no Hosoku'*, Shogakkan, 1995

—: *Zico no 'Ko' o Ikashite Katsu*, Goma Shobo, 1998